POP SOCKS
Colorful Patterns by Knit Picks

Copyright 2023 © Knit Picks

All rights reserved. This book or any portion thereof may not be reproduced or used in any manner whatsoever without the express written permission of the publisher except for the use of brief quotations in a book review.

Photography by John Cranford
Graphic Design by Lee Meredith
Content Direction by Stacey Winklepleck
Creative Direction by Hillary Elliott

Printed in the United States of America
First Printing, 2023

ISBN 978-1-62767-349-5

Versa Press, Inc.
800-447-7829
www.versapress.com

CONTENTS

Comfort DK Socks *by Renate Kamm*   8

Crosswalk Boot Socks *by Moira Engel*   12

Fallen Leaf Socks *by Weichien Chan*   18

Ghrian Ankle Socks *by Fiona Munro*   22

Making Waves Socks *by Lori Wagner*   26

No Purl Socks *by Holli Yeoh*   32

Pinner Socks *by Jo Torr*   36

Rainbow Socks *by Allison Griffith*   40

Rebound Socks *by Lauren Rose* — 44

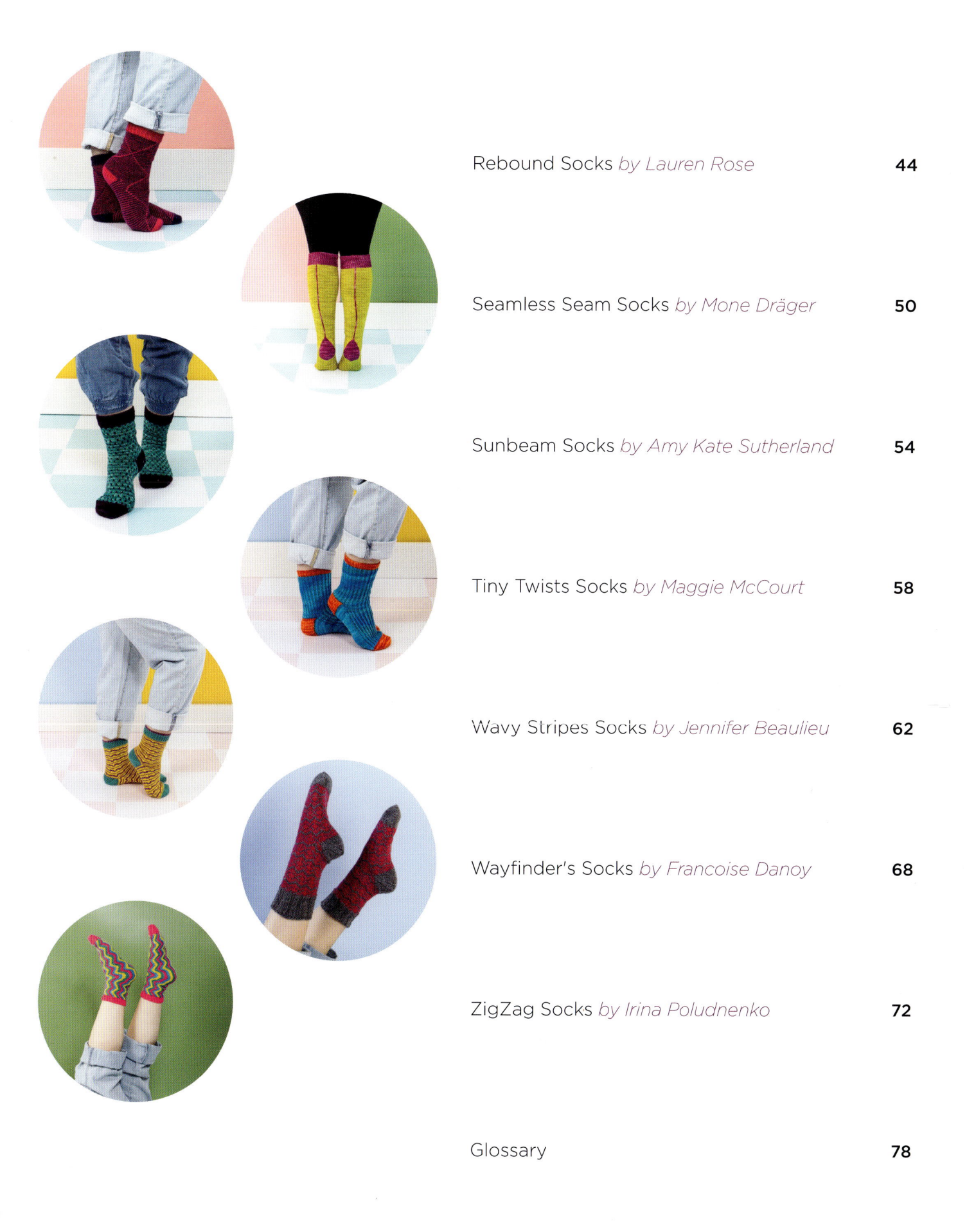

Seamless Seam Socks *by Mone Dräger* — 50

Sunbeam Socks *by Amy Kate Sutherland* — 54

Tiny Twists Socks *by Maggie McCourt* — 58

Wavy Stripes Socks *by Jennifer Beaulieu* — 62

Wayfinder's Socks *by Francoise Danoy* — 68

ZigZag Socks *by Irina Poludnenko* — 72

Glossary — 78

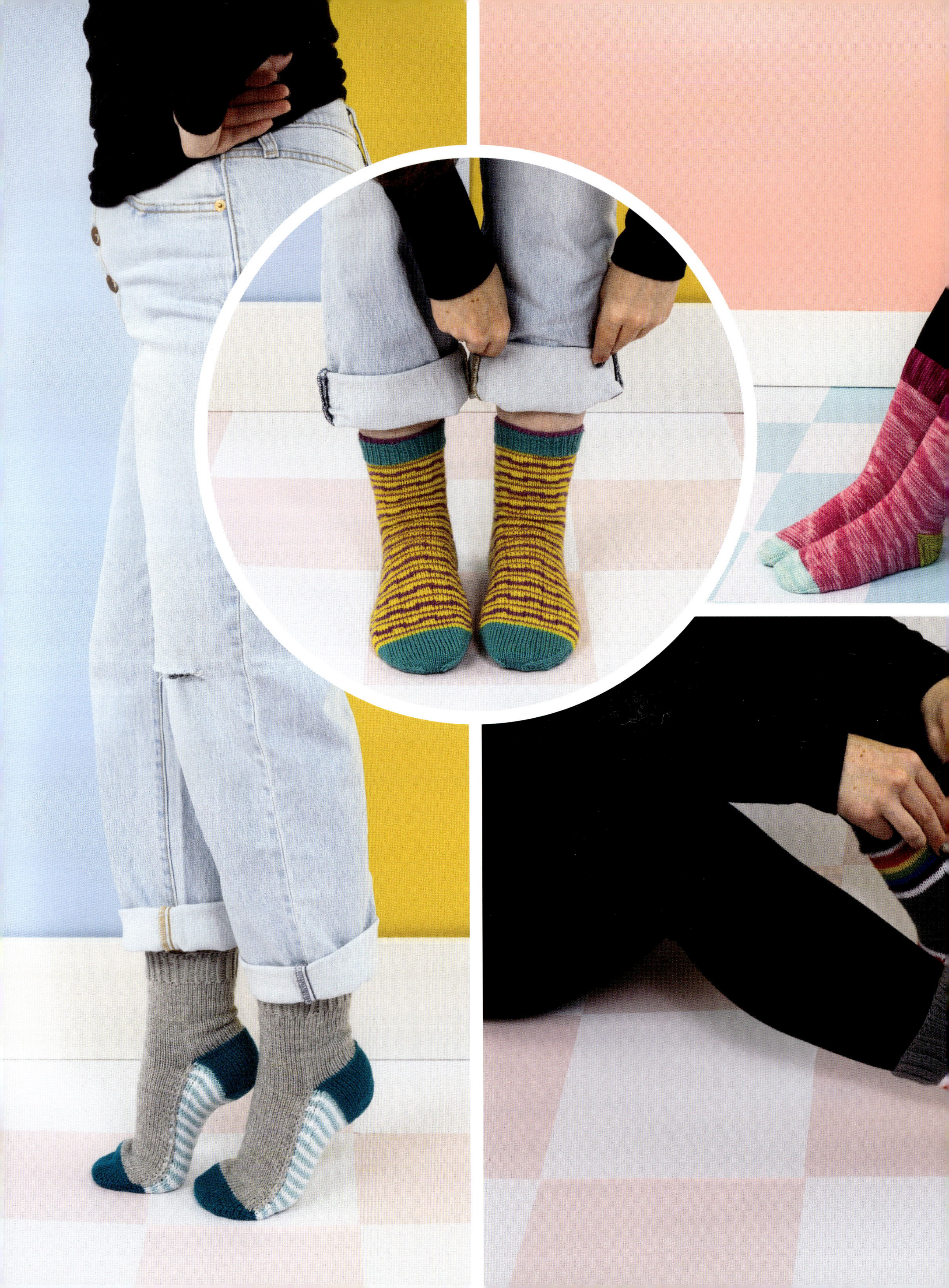

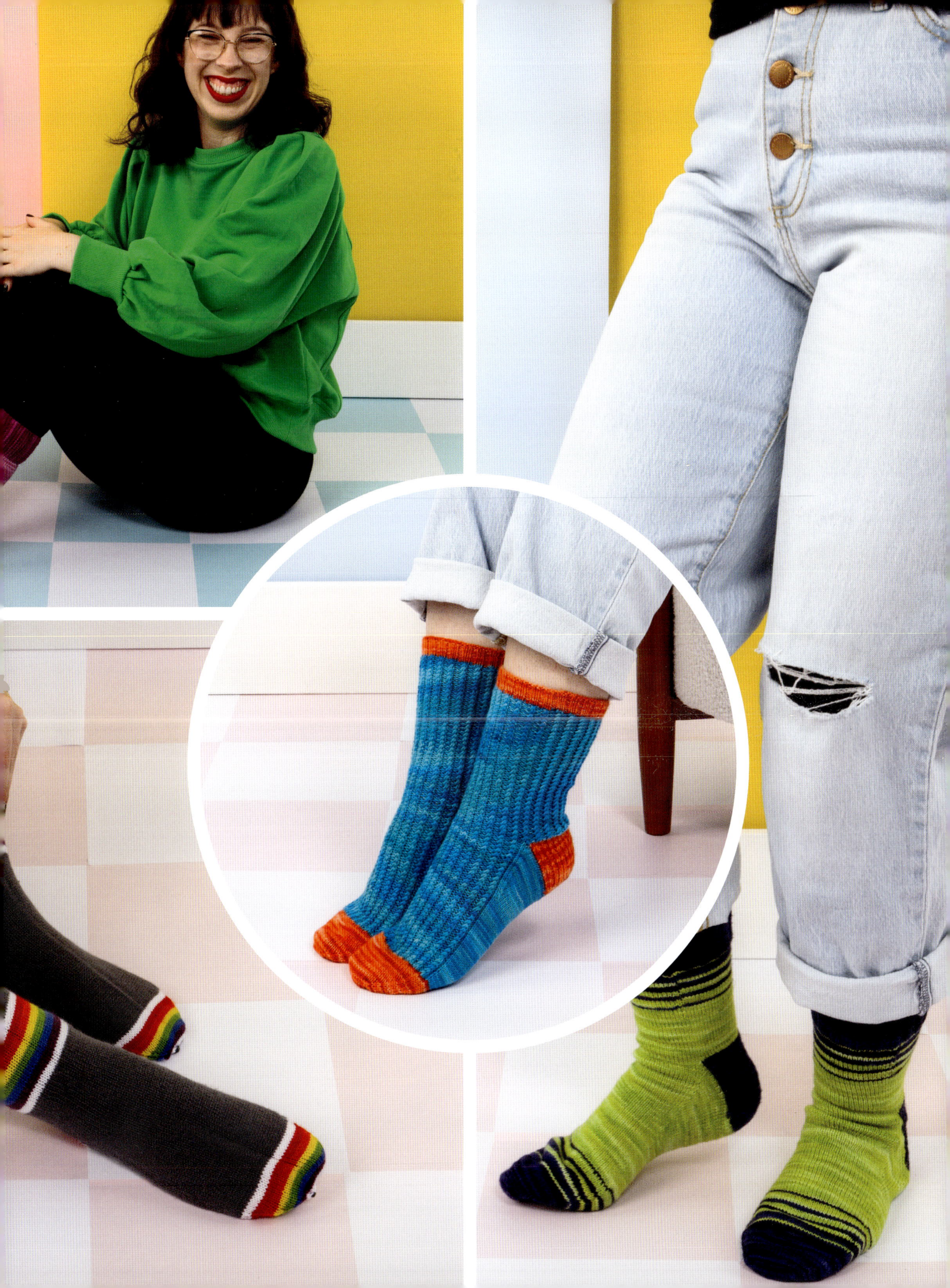

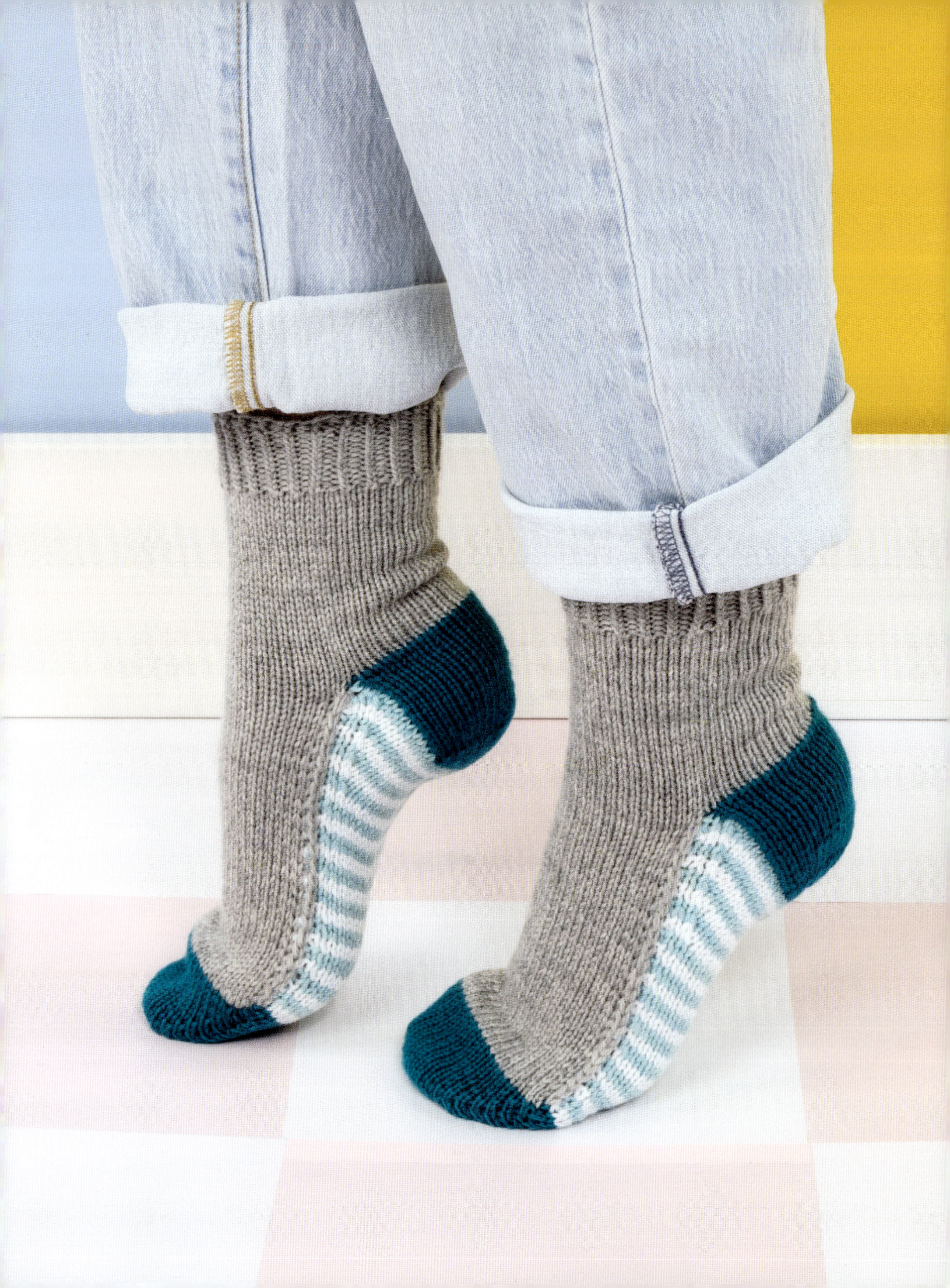

COMFORT DK SOCKS
by Renate Kamm

FINISHED MEASUREMENTS
7.5 (8.5, 9.5)" leg circumference × 8.75 (9.5, 10)" foot length; meant to be worn with approx 10% negative ease, to fit US shoe sizes 6 (8–8.5, 9.5–10)

YARN
Swish™ (DK weight, 100% Fine Superwash Merino Wool; 123 yards/50g): MC Dove Heather 24956, 1 (2, 2) skeins; C1 Marina 25578, C2 Wonderland Heather 26062, C3 White 24064, 1 skein each

NEEDLES
US 4 (3.5mm) DPNs or two circular needles for two circulars technique or 32" or longer circular needles for Magic Loop technique, or size to obtain gauge

NOTIONS
Yarn Needle
Stitch Markers
Scrap Yarn
Size G Crochet Hook

GAUGE
24 sts and 32 rnds = 4" in Stockinette Stitch, blocked

For pattern support, contact oberpfalzerin@hotmail.com

Comfort DK Socks

Notes:
The DK weight yarn makes these socks a truly quick-to-knit project. Color blocking and stripes make these Comfort DK Socks a stunner. Even though they appear to be traditional socks, an easy and not-so-traditional hybrid construction method accounts for an engaging and interesting knitting experience.

The socks start at the heel with a provisional cast on. After the heel turn, the sole is constructed in two-color, two-row stripes. Easy German Short Row toes lead to the instep, also worked in rows and joined to the sole on either side. Then all live and provisional stitches are worked in the round up to finish the leg and cuff.

Provisional Cast On (crochet chain method)
With a crochet hook, use scrap yarn to make a slip knot and chain the number of sts to be cast on, plus a few extra sts. Insert tip of knitting needle into first bump of crochet chain. Wrap project yarn around needle as if to knit, and pull yarn through crochet chain, forming first st. Rep this process until you have cast on the correct number of sts. To unravel later (when sts need to be picked up), pull chain out, leaving live sts. A photo tutorial can be found at tutorials.knitpicks.com/crocheted-provisional-cast-on.

DS (Double Stitch)
Used when working German Short Rows; see Glossary.

DIRECTIONS

Heel
With scrap yarn and crochet hook, create a chain.
With C1, provisionally CO 23 (26, 29) sts.

Heel Flap (worked flat in rows with a selvage st edge)
Row 1 (WS): WYIF Sl1 P-wise, P to end.
Row 2 (RS): WYIB Sl1 K-wise, K to end.
Rep Rows 1-2 another 9 (10, 11) times.
Rep Row 1 once more.

Heel Turn (shaped with short rows)
Short Row 1 (RS): WYIB Sl1 K-wise, K13 (14, 17), SSK, K1, turn.
Short Row 2 (WS): WYIF Sl1 P-wise, P6 (5, 8), P2tog, P1, turn.
Short Row 3 (RS): WYIB Sl1 K-wise, K to 1 st before gap, SSK, K1, turn.
Short Row 4 (WS): WYIF Sl1 P-wise, P to 1 st before gap, P2tog, P1, turn.
Rep Short Rows 3-4 another 1 (2, 2) times.
Rep Short Row 3 once more.
Final Short Row (WS): WYIF Sl1 P-wise, P to 1 st before gap, P2tog, K1 (be sure to work this last st as a knit st instead of purl). 15 (16, 19) sts.
Break C1, leaving 4" tail.

Sole
Sole is worked flat in St st, alternating C2 and C3 every two rows, with a 1-st Garter Stitch edge.
Row 1 (RS): With RS facing and live sts in left hand, join C2 at left CO heel edge, PU and K 11 (12, 13) sts (1 st in each selvage st), K across 15 (16, 19) heel sts, PU and K 11 (12, 13) sts along right side edge of heel flap (1 st in each selvage st). 37 (40, 45) sts.
Row 2 (WS): With C2, K1, P to last st, K1. Join C3.

Gusset
Decs are worked each RS row on both sides of sole to shape gussets.
Row 3 (RS): With C3, K2, SSK, K to last 4 sts, K2tog, K2. 2 sts dec.
Row 4 (WS): With C3, K1, P to last st, K1, drop C3.
Row 5: With C2, K2, SSK, K to last 4 sts, K2tog, K2. 2 sts dec.
Row 6: With C2, K1, P to last st, K1, drop C2.
Rep Rows 3-6 another 2 (2, 3) times, then rep Rows 3-4 another 1 (1, 0) time(s). 23 (26, 29) sts; 16 (16, 18) striped rows worked.

Foot
Cont two-row stripes as established, switching between C2 and C3 after every WS row.
Row 1 (RS): K across.
Row 2 (WS): K1, P to last st, K1.
Rep Rows 1-2 another 14 (14, 15) times, or until foot (heel + sole) measure approx 2 (2.25, 2.5)" shorter than desired length, ending with a WS row.
Break both C2 and C3, leaving 4" tail.

Toe
Toe is worked with C1 and German Short Rows (with double sts). Turn work to WS, slide sts to other end of needle, and join C1.
Setup Row (WS): K1, P to last st, K1.
Short rows are worked over 21 (24, 27) sts with first and last edge sts unworked.
Short Row 1 (RS): K to last st, turn.
Short Row 2 (WS): DS, P to last st, turn.
Short Row 3: DS, K to 1 st before previous DS, turn.
Short Row 4: DS, P to 1 st before previous DS, turn.
Rep Short Rows 3-4 another 5 (6, 7) times.

Next Short Row (RS): DS, (there are now 1 edge st and 8 (9, 10) DSs at each side of toe and 5 (6, 7) sts at center), K to last st (K each DS tog as 1 st), turn.
Next Short Row (WS): WYIF Sl1 P-wise, P to last st (P each DS tog as 1 st), turn.
Next Short Row: WYIB Sl1 K-wise, K13 (15, 17) sts, turn.
Next Short Row: DS, P6 (7, 8) sts, turn.
Next Short Row: DS, K to previous DS, K DS (tog as 1 st), K1, turn.
Next Short Row: DS, P to previous DS, P DS (tog as 1 st), P1, turn.
Rep last two Short Rows another 6 (7, 8) times.
Sl remaining st from RH needle to LH needle and break C1, leaving 4" tail.

Instep

Instep is worked with MC in rows and last st of each row is worked tog with its corresponding sole selvedge st, joining the two parts of the foot tog.

Row 1 (RS): Join MC, K to last st, WYIB Sl1 K-wise, with RH needle PU purl bump of first sole selvage st, K2tog TBL (K last instep st and PU loop from purl bump tog through back loop).

Row 2 (WS): WYIF Sl1 P-wise, pull yarn tightly, P to last st, WYIF Sl1 P-wise, with RH needle PU purl bump of first sole selvage st, WYIF Sl2 back to LH needle, P2tog (P last instep st and PU loop from purl bump tog).

Row 3: WYIB Sl1 P-wise, pull yarn tightly, K to last st, WYIB Sl1 K-wise, with RH needle PU purl bump of next sole selvage st, K2tog TBL.

Row 4: WYIF Sl1 P-wise, pull yarn tightly, P to last st, WYIF Sl1 P-wise, with RH needle PU purl bump of next sole selvage st, WYIF Sl2 back to LH needle, P2tog.

Rep Rows 3–4 until all sole selvage sts are joined with instep sts; last row is a WS row.

Leg

Pull out scrap yarn and Sl 22 (25, 28) sts to needle. (For Magic Loop method, Sl sts onto end of needle; for 2 circular needles method, Sl sts onto second needle; for DPNs, Sl sts onto two DPNs). Work with MC in rnds.

Setup Rnd: WYIB Sl1 K-wise, K across instep sts, K across heel sts, and PM for BOR. 45 (51, 57) sts.

Knit 32 rnds, or 1.5" shorter than desired length.

Cuff

Rnd 1: (K1, P1) to last 3 sts, K1, P2tog. 44 (50, 56) sts.

Rnd 2: (K1 TBL, P1) to end.

Rep Rnd 2 ten more times or to desired length.

Remove M and BO all sts with Jeny's Surprisingly Stretchy Bind Off (for 1x1 Rib).

Second Sock

Make second sock same as first.

Finishing

Weave in ends, wash, and block as desired.

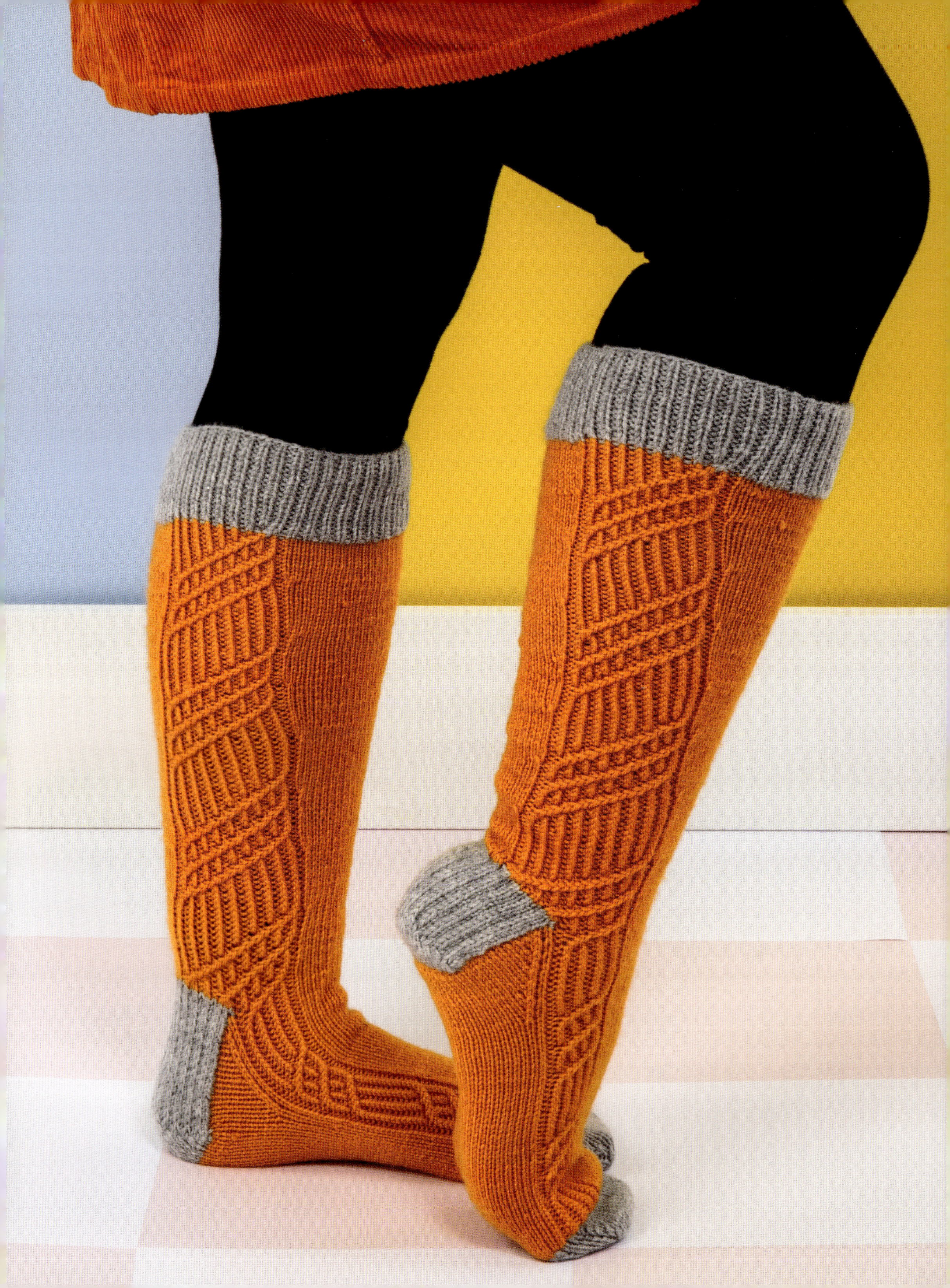

CROSSWALK BOOT SOCKS
by Moira Engel

FINISHED MEASUREMENTS
7 (8, 9)" foot circumference, 8 (11, 13)" calf circumference × 14 (15, 15)" total height; meant to be worn with 0–1" negative ease

YARN
Swish™ (DK weight, 100% Fine Superwash Merino Wool; 123 yards/50g): MC Clementine 27224, 3 (3, 4) skeins; CC Dove Heather 24956, 1 skein

NEEDLES
US 2.5 (3mm) DPNs or two circular needles for two circulars technique or 32" or longer circular needles for Magic Loop technique, or size to obtain gauge

NOTIONS
Yarn Needle
Stitch Markers
Cable Needle

GAUGE
28 sts and 36 rnds = 4" in Stockinette Stitch in the round, blocked
32 sts and 36 rnds = 4" in Crosswalk stitch patterns, blocked

For pattern support, contact bengel@telus.net

Crosswalk Boot Socks

Notes:
Crosswalk Boot Socks are a knee-high sock that is shaped at the calf and written for three sizes. Perfect for anyone: teens, ladies and men can be stylishly cozy in these unisex socks.

This is a top-down, engaging pattern suitable for the intermediate sock knitter. It's also a quick knit in a step-cushioning DK weight yarn. Pattern is for knitting in the round, with twisty cables for lots of texture.

Chart is worked in the round; read each chart row from right to left as a RS row.

1/1/1 RPT (1 over 1 Right Twist with center Purl st)
Sl2 to CN, hold in back; K1, Sl1 st from CN to LH needle and P1; K1 from CN.

1/1/1 LPT (1 over 1 Left Twist with center Purl st)
Sl2 to CN, hold in front; K1, Sl1 st from CN to LH needle and P1; K1 from CN.

Chart A (in the round over 19 sts)
Rnd 1: (P1, K1 TBL) seven times, P1, 1/1/1 RPT, P1.
Rnd 2 and all even rounds: (P1, K1 TBL) nine times, P1.
Rnd 3: (P1, K1 TBL) six times, P1, 1/1/1 RPT, P1, K1 TBL, P1.
Rnd 5: (P1, K1 TBL) five times, P1, 1/1/1 RPT, (P1, K1 TBL) two times, P1.
Rnd 7: (P1, K1 TBL) four times, P1, 1/1/1 RPT, P1, K1 TBL, P1, 1/1/1 RPT, P1.
Rnd 9: (P1, K1 TBL) three times, (P1, 1/1/1 RPT, P1, K1 TBL) two times, P1.
Rnd 11: (P1, K1 TBL) two times, (P1, 1/1/1 RPT, P1, K1 TBL) two times, P1, K1 TBL, P1.
Rnd 13: (P1, K1 TBL, P1, 1/1/1 RPT) three times, P1.
Rnd 15: (P1, 1/1/1 RPT, P1, K1 TBL) three times, P1.
Rnd 17: Rep Rnd 11.
Rnd 19: (P1, K1 TBL, P1, 1/1/1 RPT) two times, (P1, K1 TBL) three times, P1.
Rnd 21: (P1, 1/1/1 RPT, P1, K1 TBL) two times, (P1, K1 TBL) four times, P1.
Rnd 23: (P1, K1 TBL) two times, P1, 1/1/1 RPT, (P1, K1 TBL) five times, P1.
Rnd 25: P1, K1 TBL, P1, 1/1/1 RPT, (P1, K1 TBL) six times, P1.
Rnd 27: P1, 1/1/1 RPT, (P1, K1 TBL) seven times, P1.
Rnd 28: Rep Rnd 2.
Rep Rnds 1-28 for pattern.

Chart A Foot (in the round over 9 sts)
Rnd 1: (P1, K1 TBL) two times, P1, 1/1/1 RPT, P1.
Rnd 2: (P1, K1 TBL) four times, P1.
Rnd 3: P1, K1 TBL, P1, 1/1/1 RPT, P1, K1 TBL, P1.
Rnd 4: Rep Rnd 2.
Rnd 5: P1, 1/1/1 RPT, (P1, K1 TBL) two times, P1.
Rnd 6: Rep Rnd 2.
Rnds 7-18: Rep Rnds 1-6.
Rnds 19-28: (P1, K1 TBL) four times, P1.
Rep Rnds 1-28 for pattern.

Chart B (in the round over 19 sts)
Rnd 1: P1, 1/1/1 LPT, (P1, K1 TBL) seven times, P1.
Rnd 2 and all even rnds: (P1, K1 TBL) nine times, P1.
Rnd 3: P1, K1 TBL, P1, 1/1/1 LPT, (P1, K1 TBL) six times, P1.
Rnd 5: (P1, K1 TBL) two times, P1, 1/1/1 LPT, (P1, K1 TBL) five times, P1.
Rnd 7: (P1, 1/1/1 LPT, P1, K1 TBL) two times, (P1, K1 TBL) three times, P1.
Rnd 9: (P1, K1 TBL, P1, 1/1/1 LPT) two times, (P1, K1 TBL) three times, P1.
Rnd 11: P1, K1 TBL, (P1, K1 TBL, P1, 1/1/1 LPT) two times, (P1, K1 TBL) two times, P1.
Rnd 13: (P1, 1/1/1 LPT, P1, K1 TBL) three times, P1.
Rnd 15: (P1, K1 TBL, P1, 1/1/1 LPT) three times, P1.
Rnd 17: Rep Rnd 11.
Rnd 19: (P1, K1 TBL) three times, (P1, 1/1/1 LPT, P1, K1 TBL) two times, P1.
Rnd 21: (P1, K1 TBL) four times, P1, 1/1/1 LPT, P1, K1 TBL, P1, 1/1/1 LPT, P1.
Rnd 23: (P1, K1 TBL) five times, P1, 1/1/1 LPT, (P1, K1 TBL) two times, P1.
Rnd 25: (P1, K1 TBL) six times, P1, 1/1/1 LPT, P1, K1 TBL, P1.
Rnd 27: (P1, K1 TBL) seven times, P1, 1/1/1 LPT, P1.
Rnd 28: Rep Rnd 2.
Rep Rnds 1-28 for pattern.

Chart B Foot (in the round over 9 sts)
Rnd 1: P1, 1/1/1 LPT, (P1, K1 TBL) two times, P1.
Rnd 2: (P1, K1 TBL) four times, P1.
Rnd 3: P1, K1 TBL, P1, 1/1/1 LPT, P1, K1 TBL, P1.
Rnd 4: Rep Rnd 2.
Rnd 5: (P1, K1 TBL) two times, P1, 1/1/1 LPT, P1.
Rnd 6: Rep Rnd 2.
Rnds 7-18: Rep Rnds 1-6.
Rnds 19-28: (P1, K1 TBL) four times, P1.
Rep Rnds 1-28 for pattern.

DIRECTIONS

Leg
With CC, CO 64 (88, 104) sts. Join to work in the rnd; PM for BOR, which is oriented to the back, just before where Chart A will begin after ribbing is complete.
Setup Rnd: (P1, K1) nine times, P1, PM, (K1, P1) 6 (12, 16) times, K1, PM, (P1, K1) nine times, P1, PM, (K1, P1) 6 (12, 16) times, K1. Work 1x1 Rib as established for 2".
Change to MC.
Next Rnd: Work Chart A, SM, K13 (25, 33) to M, work Chart B, SM, K13 (25, 33) to end.
Cont in pattern as established and at the same time work Dec Rnd every 22 (12, 11) rnds 4 (7, 8) times.
Dec Rnd: Work Chart A, SM, K2tog, K to 2 sts before M, SSK, SM, work Chart B, SM, K2tog, K to 2 sts before BOR, SSK.
4 sts dec.
16 (28, 32) sts dec. 48 (60, 72) remain.

WE as established until sock measures 12 (12.5, 12)" from CO edge. Make note of which pattern rnd was worked last.

Heel Flap
Change to CC.
Heel Setup: K10, turn. P25 (31, 37), turn. These 25 (31, 37) sts will form heel flap. Remove BOR M.
Row 1 (RS): (Sl1, K1) 12 (15, 18) times, K1.
Row 2 (WS): P25 (31, 37).
Rep Rows 1–2 until heel flap measures 2 (2.5, 3)", ending after a RS row.

Heel Turn
Short Row 1 (WS): P16 (20, 24), P2tog, P1, turn. 24 (30, 36) sts.
Short Row 2 (RS): Sl1, K8 (10, 12), SSK, K1, turn. 23 (29, 35) sts.
Short Row 3: Sl1, P to 1 st before gap, P2tog, P1, turn. 1 st dec.
Short Row 4: Sl1, K to 1 st before gap, SSK, K1, turn. 1 st dec.
Rep Short Rows 3–4 another 2 (3, 4) times. Do not turn after last RS row. 17 (21, 25) sts.

Gusset
Setup: Continuing from heel, change to MC, PU and K 10 (12, 14) sts along heel flap edge, PM for new BOR, work 9-st Chart A Foot beginning on next pattern rnd after the one noted before heel, SM, K5 (11, 17), SM, work 9-st Chart B Foot beginning on same pattern rnd, PM, PU and K 10 (12, 14) sts along opposite heel flap edge, work to end. 60 (74, 88) sts.

Rnd 1: Work as established to M after Chart B Foot, SM, K1, SSK, K to last 3 sts, K2tog, K1. 2 sts dec.
Rnd 2: WE as established.
Rep Rnds 1–2 another 6 (7, 8) times. 46 (58, 70) sts.

Foot
WE as established until foot measures 7.5 (8.25, 8.75)" or desired length from back of heel.

Toe
Setup: K23 (29, 35) PM for side, K to end.
Rnd 1: (K1, K2tog, K to 3 sts before M, SSK, K1, SM) two times. 4 sts dec.
Rnd 2: K all.
Rep Rnds 1–2 another 5 (7, 9) times. 22 (26, 30) sts.
Graft remaining sts tog.

Second Sock
Make second sock same as first.

Finishing
Weave in ends, wash, and block as desired.

Chart A

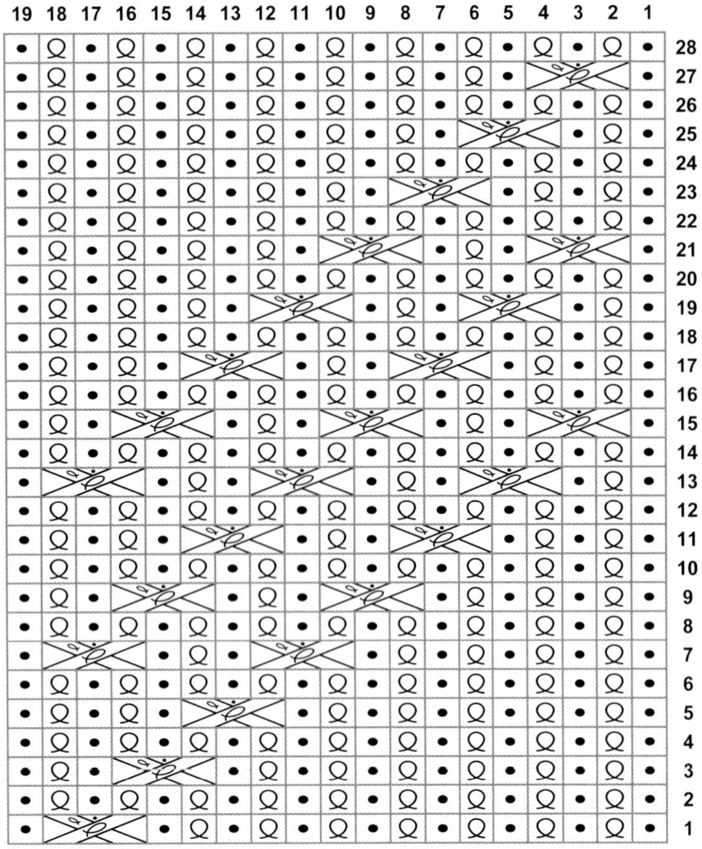

Chart B

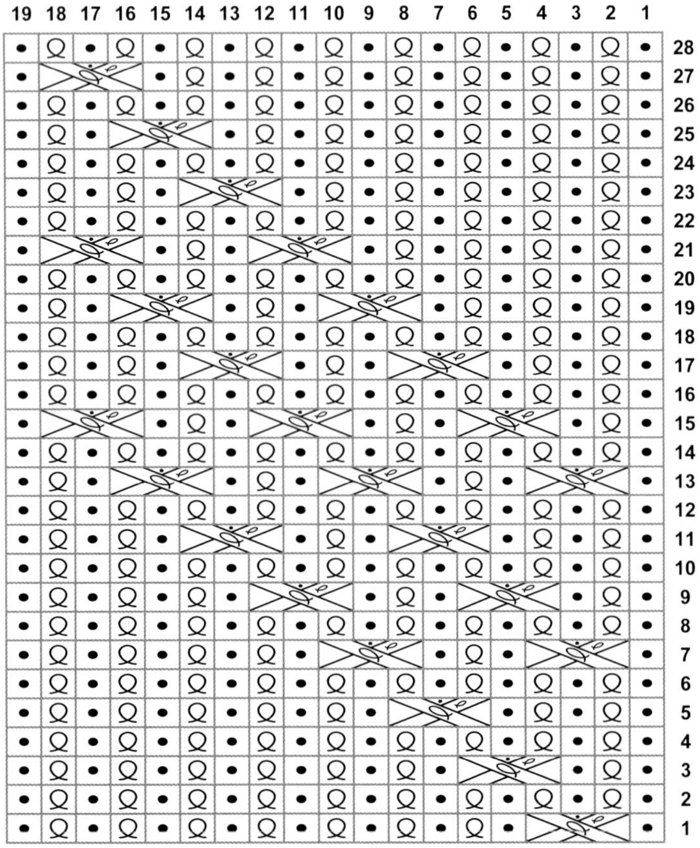

LEGEND

Purl Stitch

K TBL
Knit stitch through the back loop

1 over 1 over 1 Left Twist, Purl center (1/1/1 LPT)
Sl2 to CN, hold in front; K1, Sl1 st from CN to LH needle and P1; K1 from CN

1 over 1 over 1 Right Twist, Purl center (1/1/1 RPT)
Sl2 to CN, hold in back; K1, Sl1 st from CN to LH needle and P1; K1 from CN

WE as established until sock measures 12 (12.5, 12)" from CO edge. Make note of which pattern rnd was worked last.

Heel Flap
Change to CC.
Heel Setup: K10, turn. P25 (31, 37), turn. These 25 (31, 37) sts will form heel flap. Remove BOR M.
Row 1 (RS): (Sl1, K1) 12 (15, 18) times, K1.
Row 2 (WS): P25 (31, 37).
Rep Rows 1-2 until heel flap measures 2 (2.5, 3)", ending after a RS row.

Heel Turn
Short Row 1 (WS): P16 (20, 24), P2tog, P1, turn. 24 (30, 36) sts.
Short Row 2 (RS): Sl1, K8 (10, 12), SSK, K1, turn. 23 (29, 35) sts.
Short Row 3: Sl1, P to 1 st before gap, P2tog, P1, turn. 1 st dec.
Short Row 4: Sl1, K to 1 st before gap, SSK, K1, turn. 1 st dec.
Rep Short Rows 3-4 another 2 (3, 4) times. Do not turn after last RS row. 17 (21, 25) sts.

Gusset
Setup: Continuing from heel, change to MC, PU and K 10 (12, 14) sts along heel flap edge, PM for new BOR, work 9-st Chart A Foot beginning on next pattern rnd after the one noted before heel, SM, K5 (11, 17), SM, work 9-st Chart B Foot beginning on same pattern rnd, PM, PU and K 10 (12, 14) sts along opposite heel flap edge, work to end. 60 (74, 88) sts.

Rnd 1: Work as established to M after Chart B Foot, SM, K1, SSK, K to last 3 sts, K2tog, K1. 2 sts dec.
Rnd 2: WE as established.
Rep Rnds 1-2 another 6 (7, 8) times. 46 (58, 70) sts.

Foot
WE as established until foot measures 7.5 (8.25, 8.75)" or desired length from back of heel.

Toe
Setup: K23 (29, 35) PM for side, K to end.
Rnd 1: (K1, K2tog, K to 3 sts before M, SSK, K1, SM) two times. 4 sts dec.
Rnd 2: K all.
Rep Rnds 1-2 another 5 (7, 9) times. 22 (26, 30) sts.
Graft remaining sts tog.

Second Sock
Make second sock same as first.

Finishing
Weave in ends, wash, and block as desired.

Chart A

Chart B

LEGEND

- • Purl Stitch

- Q   K TBL
  Knit stitch through the back loop

- **1 over 1 over 1 Left Twist, Purl center (1/1/1 LPT)**
  Sl2 to CN, hold in front; K1, Sl1 st from CN to LH needle and P1; K1 from CN

- **1 over 1 over 1 Right Twist, Purl center (1/1/1 RPT)**
  Sl2 to CN, hold in back; K1, Sl1 st from CN to LH needle and P1; K1 from CN

16   Crosswalk Boot Socks

Chart A Foot

Chart B Foot

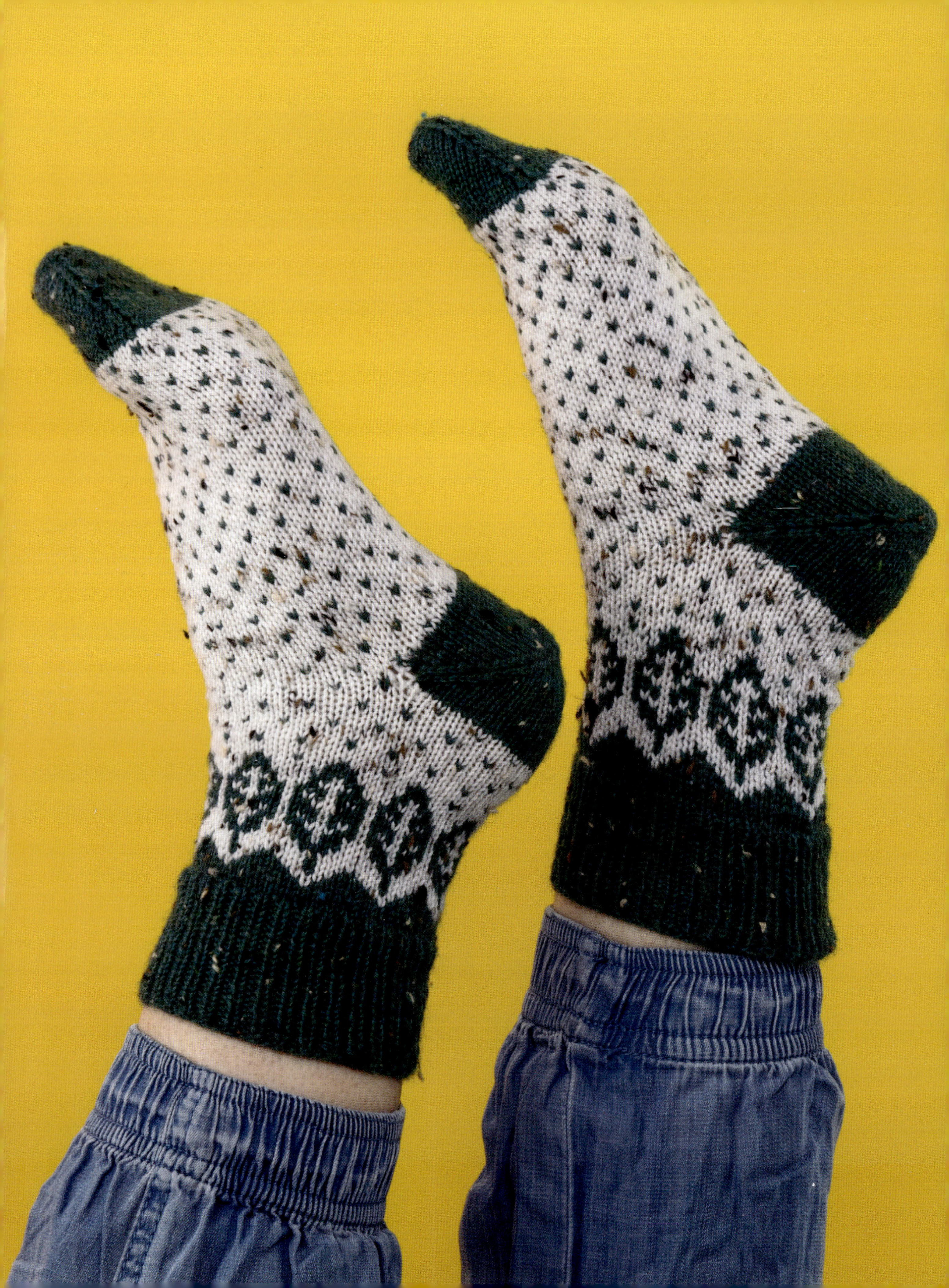

FALLEN LEAF SOCKS
by Weichien Chan

FINISHED MEASUREMENTS
4.5 (5.5, 6, 6.5, 7, 8)(9, 10, 11, 12, 12.5)" leg circumference × 4.75 (5.5, 6.75, 7.5, 8.25, 9.5)(10.25, 11, 12.5, 13, 13)" foot length; meant to be worn with approx 10% negative ease, to fit US shoe sizes 4.5C (5C–7.5C, 8C–11C, 11.5C–13.5C, 4.5–6, 6.5–8.5)(9–11.5, 12–14.5, 15–15.5, 16–16.5, 17)

YARN
Stroll™ Tweed (fingering weight, 65% Fine Superwash Merino Wool, 25% Nylon, 10% Donegal Tweed; 231 yards/50g): MC Atlantis Heather 28192, CC Dalmatian 28188, 1 (1, 1, 1, 1, 1)(1, 2, 2, 2, 2) skeins each

NEEDLES
US 1 (2.25mm) DPNs or 32" or longer circular needles for Magic Loop technique, or size to obtain gauge

NOTIONS
Yarn Needle
Stitch Markers
Scrap Yarn

GAUGE
33 sts and 40 rnds = 4" in Stranded Stockinette Stitch in the round, blocked

For pattern support, contact hello@thepetiteknitter.com

Fallen Leaf Socks

Fallen Leaf Socks

Notes:

Shift into the new season and embrace all the cozy, hygge, and autumnal vibes with the Fallen Leaf Socks.

Fallen Leaf are top-down socks, worked in the round. They have colorwork around the legs and light colorwork throughout. The socks feature an afterthought heel and use grafting for finishing.

Instructions are both written and charted. Chart is worked in the round; read each chart row from right to left as a RS row. Knit all stitches on chart.

Fallen Leaf Pattern (in the round over 8 sts)
Rnd 1: With MC, K all.
Rnd 2: Rep Rnd 1.
Rnd 3: (With MC, K3; with CC, K1; with MC, K4) to end.
Rnd 4: (With MC, K2; with CC, K3; with MC, K3) to end.
Rnd 5: (With MC, K1; with CC, K2; with MC, K1; with CC, K2; with MC, K2) to end.
Rnd 6: (With CC, K3; with MC, K1) to end.
Rnd 7: (With CC, K3; with MC, K1; with CC, K4) to end.
Rnd 8: (With CC, K2; with MC, K3; with CC, K3) to end.
Rnd 9: (With CC, K1; with MC, K2; with CC, K1; with MC, K2; with CC, K2) to end.
Rnd 10: Rep Rnd 9.
Rnd 11: (With MC, K2; with CC, K3; with MC, K2; with CC, K1) to end.
Rnd 12: (With MC, K1; with CC, K1) to end.
Rnd 13: (With MC, K3; with CC, K1) to end.
Rnd 14: Rep Rnd 11.
Rnd 15: Rep Rnd 12.
Rnd 16: Rep Rnd 13.
Rnd 17: (With CC, K1; with MC, K2; with CC, K1; with MC, K2; with CC, K2) to end.
Rnd 18: Rep Rnd 9.
Rnd 19: Rep Rnd 8.
Rnd 20: Rep Rnd 19.
Rnd 21: (With CC, K3; with MC, K1) to end.
Rnd 22: With CC, K all.
Rnd 23: Rep Rnd 22.
Rnd 24: (With CC, K3; with MC, K1) to end.
Rnd 25: With CC, K all.
Rnd 26: Rep Rnd 25.
Rnd 27: (With CC, K1; with MC, K1; with CC, K3; with MC, K1; with CC, K2) to end.
Rnd 28: With CC, K all.
Rep Rnds 23-28 for pattern.

DIRECTIONS

Cuff
Using MC, loosely CO 40 (48, 48, 56, 56, 64)(72, 80, 88, 96, 104) sts. Join to work in the rnd, being careful not to twist sts; PM for BOR.
Work 1x1 Rib until work measures 2" from CO edge.

Leg
Setup Rnd: K all.

Work Fallen Leaf Pattern from chart or written instructions, completing Rnds 1-28.
Rep Rnds 23-28 until work measures 3.25 (3.25, 3.25, 4.5, 4.5, 5.5)(5.5, 5.5, 5.5, 5.5, 5.5)" from end of ribbing.
When desired length is reached, be sure to end on a plain CC rnd (Rnd 25 or 28).

Heel Opening
Using scrap yarn, K20 (24, 24, 28, 28, 32)(36, 40, 44, 48, 52), Sl scrap yarn sts back onto LH needle.

Foot
Cont working pattern as established, rep Rnds 23-28 until work measures 2 (2.25, 3.25, 3.5, 4.25, 5)(5.5, 6.25, 7, 7.5, 7.5)" from heel opening or 2.75 (3.25, 3.25, 4, 4, 4.5)(4.75, 4.75, 5.5, 5.5, 5.5)" shorter than desired foot length.
When desired length is reached, be sure to end on a plain CC rnd (Rnd 25 or 28).

Toe
Toe is worked in the rnd in MC. PM after 20 (24, 24, 28, 28, 32)(36, 40, 44, 48, 52) sts.
Rnd 1: (SSK, K to 2 sts before M, K2tog) two times. 4 sts dec.
Rnd 2: K all.
Rep Rnds 1-2 another 4 (5, 5, 6, 6, 7)(7, 7, 7, 7, 7) times. 20 (24, 24, 28, 28, 32)(40, 48, 56, 64, 72) sts.
Rep Rnd 1 another 3 (4, 4, 5, 5, 5)(6, 8, 9, 9, 9) times. 8 (8, 8, 8, 8, 12)(16, 16, 20, 28, 36) sts.

Break yarn, leaving a 12" tail. Graft sts tog.

Afterthought Heel
Heel is worked in the rnd using MC. Remove scrap yarn. Place 20 (24, 24, 28, 28, 32)(36, 40, 44, 48, 52) leg sts on one needle; place 20 (24, 24, 28, 28, 32)(36, 40, 44, 48, 52) foot sts on one needle.

Attach MC, leaving a tail of at least 6".
Setup Rnd 1: *PU and K 1 st, K to end of leg sts, PU and K 1 st, PM; rep from * once more for foot sts (second M is BOR). If desired, twist picked up corner sts to eliminate holes.
44 (52, 52, 60, 60, 68)(76, 84, 92, 100, 108) sts total.
Setup Rnd 2: K all.

Heel Decreases
Rnd 1: (SSK, K to 2 sts before M, K2tog) two times. 4 sts dec.
Rnd 2: K all.

Fallen Leaf Pattern

	8	7	6	5	4	3	2	1	
									28
			■				■		27
									26
									25
			■				■		24
									23
									22
	■								21
				■					20
				■	■				19
				■	■				18
									17
		■	■		■	■			16
		■		■		■			15
									14
									13
									12
				■					11
			■	■	■				10
			■	■	■				9
		■				■			8
						■			7
	■	■					■		6
									5
									4
									3
									2
									1

LEGEND

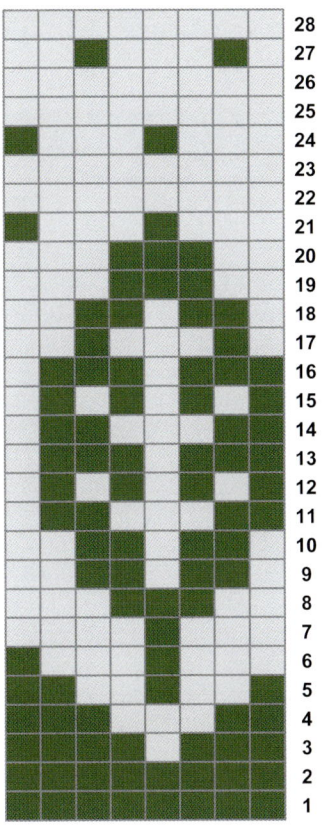

- ■ Main Color
- ▨ Contrasting Color
- ☐ Knit Stitch

Rep Rnds 1–2 another 5 (6, 6, 7, 7, 8)(9, 10, 11, 11, 11) times. 20 (24, 24, 28, 28, 32)(36, 40, 44, 52, 60) sts. Rep Rnd 1 another 2 (3, 3, 4, 4, 4)(5, 5, 6, 8, 8) times. 12 (12, 12, 12, 12, 16)(16, 20, 20, 20, 28) sts.

Finishing

Break yarn, leaving a long tail. With yarn needle, graft sts tog.

Weave in ends, wash, and block as desired.

Second Sock

Make second sock same as first.

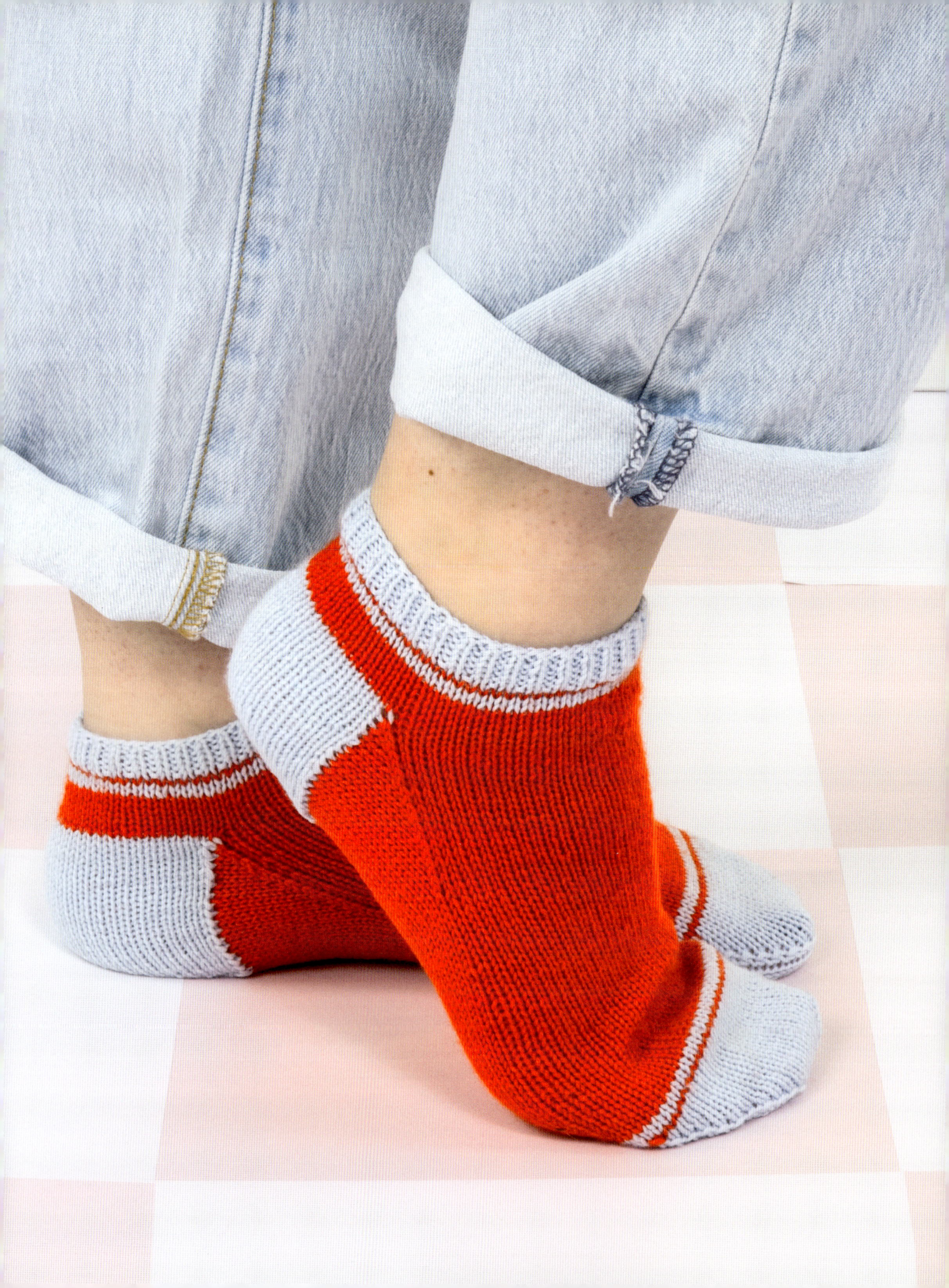

GHRIAN ANKLE SOCKS
by Fiona Munro

FINISHED MEASUREMENTS
6 (7, 8, 9, 10)" leg circumference × 9.75 (10, 10.25, 10.5, 10.75)" foot length; meant to be worn with 0.5" negative ease, to fit US shoe sizes 6 (7, 8, 9, 10)

YARN
Stroll™ (fingering weight, 75% Fine Superwash Merino Wool, 25% Nylon; 231 yards/50g): MC Frost 28183, CC Buoy 28180, 1 skein each

NEEDLES
US 1.5 (2.5mm) DPNs or two circular needles for two circulars technique or 32" or longer circular needles for Magic Loop technique, or size to obtain gauge

NOTIONS
Yarn Needle
Stitch Markers

GAUGE
32 sts and 40 rnds = 4" in Stockinette Stitch in the round, blocked
40 sts and 48 rnds = 4" in 1x1 Rib in the round, blocked (note that this is approximate due to the amount of stretch in the ribbing)

For pattern support, contact munrosisters3@gmail.com

Ghrian Ankle Socks

Notes:

These bright and playful socks are inspired by rays of sunshine against bright blue skies, which is why these are called ghrian, the Gaelic word for sun.

These ankle socks are worked from the top down with two colors of yarn that show off the ankle ribbing, heel, and toe. The heel is worked as a flap and gusset heel, and the toe is grafted as a wedge toe.

DIRECTIONS

Cuff
With MC, CO 48 (56, 64, 72, 80) sts. Join to work in the rnd, being careful not to twist sts; PM for BOR.

Work 1x1 Rib until piece measures 0.5" from CO edge.

Leg
With CC, knit one rnd.
With MC, knit two rnds.
With CC, knit until piece measures 1.5" from CO edge.

Heel Flap
The heel is worked in MC only, on first 24 (28, 32, 36, 40) sts.
Row 1 (RS): Sl1 WYIB, K23 (27, 31, 35, 39), turn.
Row 2 (WS): Sl1 WYIF, P23 (27, 31, 35, 39), turn.
Rep Rows 1-2 another 11 (13, 15, 17, 19) times.

Heel Turn
Short Row 1 (RS): K14 (16, 19, 21, 23), SSK, K1, turn. 23 (27, 31, 35, 39) heel sts.
Short Row 2 (WS): Sl1 WYIF, P5 (5, 7, 7, 7), P2tog, P1, turn. 22 (26, 30, 34, 38) heel sts.
Short Row 3: Sl1 WYIB, K to 1 st before gap, SSK, K1, turn. 1 st dec.
Short Row 4: Sl1WYIF, P to 1 st before gap, P2tog, P1, turn. 1 st dec.
Rep Short Rows 3-4 another 2 (3, 4, 5, 6) times. 16 (18, 20, 22, 24) sts.

Sizes 6 (7, -, -, -)" Only
Next Short Row (RS): Sl1 WYIB, K to 1 st before gap, SSK, turn. 1 st dec.
Next Short Row (WS): Sl1 WYIF, P to 1 st before gap, P2tog. 14 (16, -, -, -) sts.

Gusset
With CC, K14 (16, 20, 22, 24) heel sts, PU and K 12 (14, 16, 18, 20) sts along edge of heel flap, K24 (28, 32, 36, 40), PU and K 12 (14, 16, 18, 20) sts along edge of heel flap. 62 (72, 84, 94, 104) sts.

Dec Rnd: K to 2 sts before instep, K2tog, K instep sts; SSK, K to end. 2 sts dec.
Work St st and rep Dec Rnd every other rnd 6 (7, 9, 10, 11) more times. 48 (56, 64, 72, 80) sts.

Foot
With CC, work St st until sock measures 7 (7, 7.25, 7.5, 7.75)" or 2.25 (2.5, 2.5, 2.5, 2.5)" shorter than desired foot length, ending final rnd at start of instep sts.

With MC, knit two rnds.
With CC, knit one rnd. Break CC.

Toe
Toe is worked in MC.
Rnd 1: K1, SSK, K to 3 sts before end of instep, K2tog, K2, SSK, K to last 3 sts, K2tog, K1. 4 sts dec.
Rnd 2: K all.
Rep Rnds 1-2 another 8 (10, 10, 10, 10) times. 12 (12, 20, 28, 36) sts.

Break yarn, leaving a 12" tail. Graft toe sts closed.

Second Sock
Make second sock same as first.

Finishing
To block, wash the socks. Stretching on sock blockers is not required. Weave in ends once dry.

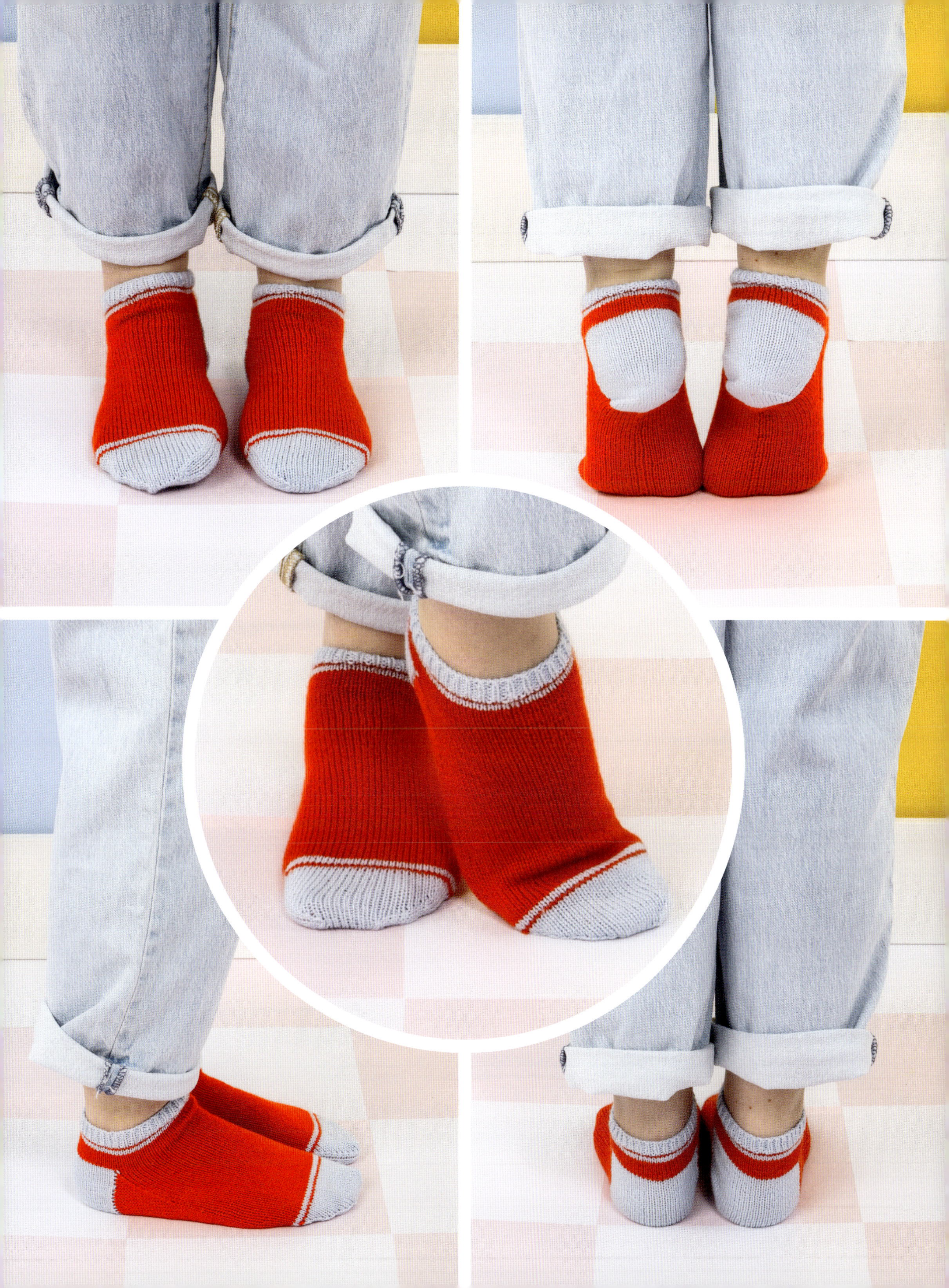

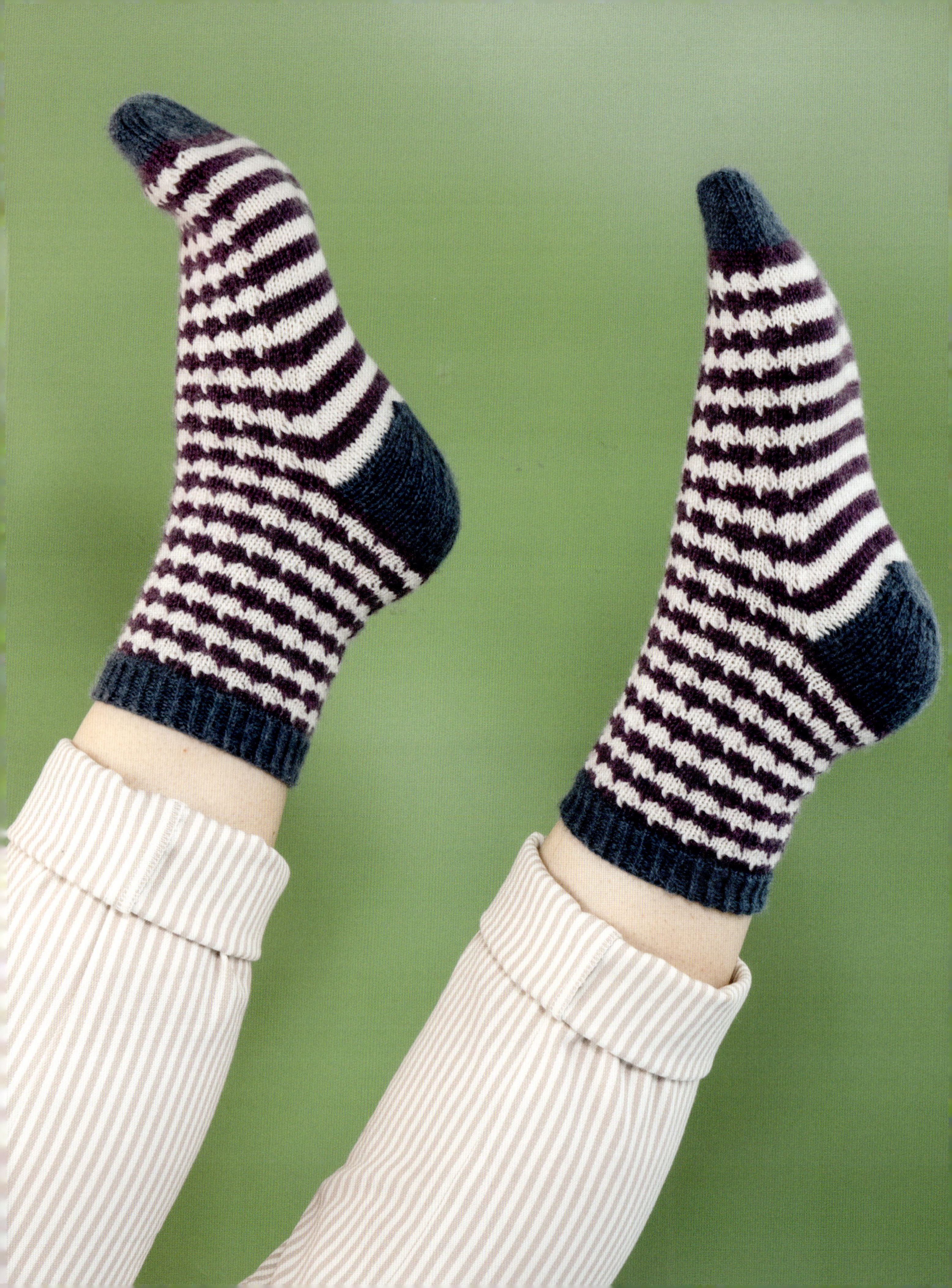

MAKING WAVES SOCKS
by Lori Wagner

FINISHED MEASUREMENTS
7.25 (8.25, 9.25)" foot circumference × 7.5 (8.5, 9.5)" leg length; foot length is adjustable; meant to be worn with 10% negative ease

YARN
Capretta™ (fingering weight, 80% Fine Superwash Merino Wool, 10% Cashmere, 10% Nylon; 230 yards/50g): C1 Loganberry Heather 27646, C2 White 27633, C3 Adriatic Heather 27645, 1 ball each

NEEDLES
US 1 (2.25mm) DPNs or two circular needles for two circulars technique or 40" or longer circular needles for Magic Loop technique, or size used to obtain gauge

NOTIONS
Yarn Needle
Removable Stitch Marker

GAUGE
32 sts and 48 rnds = 4" in Stockinette Stitch in the round, blocked
30 sts and 48 rnds = 4" in Making Waves Pattern in the round, blocked
34 sts and 43 rnds = 4" in 1x1 Twisted Rib in the round, blocked (note that this is approximate due to the amount of stretch in the ribbing)

For pattern support, contact davenlori98@hotmail.com

Making Waves Socks

Notes:
Like the undulating ocean waves rolling, creating a rhythmically relaxing sound, the Making Waves Socks mimic this with the needles. A soothing four-stripe repeat, with one of those rows using a Dip Stitch, is sure to keep interest in working just one more row!

Making Waves Socks is top-down gusset sock that uses two colors for the Making Waves striping pattern and a third color for the top ribbing, heel flap, and toe.

After working the Dip Stitch, the stitch to the left might look loose and the Dip Stitch tight. To tidy up the two stitches, use the tip of one needle and lightly pull on the left leg of the Dip Stitch; to even out the other stitch, carefully pull on its right leg.

When working the Making Waves stitch pattern using the two colors, the non-working color can be carried up the side by twisting it around the working yarn every other row.

Always slip stitches purl-wise.

Picking Up Stitches
When picking up sts along the heel flap, insert needle tip under both legs of the slipped st along edge of heel flap, wrap yarn around needle K-wise and pull through onto RH needle. Cont this along edge of heel flap.

Dip (Dip Stitch)
Insert RH needle into front of the third st below next st on LH needle, and draw up loop; then K the next st on LH needle and pass loop over the st just knitted.

1x1 Twisted Rib (in the round over an even number of sts)
Rnd 1: (K1 TBL, P1) to end.
Rep Rnd 1 for pattern.

Making Waves Right (in the round over a multiple of 4 sts)
Rnd 1: With C1, K all.
Rnd 2: Rep Rnd 1.
Rnd 3: Rep Rnd 1.
Rnd 4: With C2, (K3, Dip) to end.
Rnd 5: With C2, K all.
Rnd 6: Rep Rnd 5.
Rnd 7: Rep Rnd 5.
Rnd 8: With C1, K1, (Dip, K3) to last 3 sts, Dip, K2.
Rep Rnds 1–8 for pattern.

Making Waves Left (in the round over a multiple of 4 sts)
Rnd 1: With C1, K all.
Rnd 2: Rep Rnd 1.
Rnd 3: Rep Rnd 1.
Rnd 4: With C2, (Dip, K3) to end.
Rnd 5: With C2, K all.
Rnd 6: Rep Rnd 5.
Rnd 7: Rep Rnd 5.
Rnd 8: With C1, K2, (Dip, K3) to last 2 sts, Dip, K1.
Rep Rnds 1–8 for pattern.

DIRECTIONS

Cuff
Using C3 and Long Tail Cast On, loosely CO 56 (64, 72) sts. Join to work in rnd, being careful not to twist sts; PM for BOR.
Work 1x1 Twisted Rib for twelve rnds.
Knit one rnd. Break C3.

Right Leg
Work Rnds 1–8 of Making Waves Right pattern seven times. Work pattern Rnds 1–3 once more. Do not break C1 or C2.

Heel Flap
Heel is worked back and forth on next 28 (32, 36) sts using C3. Rearrange sts on needles as preferred. Remaining 28 (32, 36) sts will be worked later for instep.

Setup Row (RS): With C3, K28 (32, 36) sts, turn.
Row 1 (WS): (Sl1 WYIF, P1) to end of heel sts.
Row 2: Sl1 WYIB, K to end of heel sts.
Rep Rows 1–2 another 15 (17, 17) times.
Rep Row 1 once more. 32 (36, 36) rows total; 16 (18, 18) selvage sts.

Heel Turn
Work short rows to shape heel as follows.
Short Row 1 (RS): With C3, Sl1 WYIB, K16 (18, 20), SSK, K1, turn. 1 st dec.
Short Row 2 (WS): Sl1 WYIF, P7, P2tog, P1, turn. 1 st dec.
Short Row 3: Sl1WYIB, K to 1 st before gap, SSK (1 st from each side of gap), K1, turn. 1 st dec.
Short Row 4: Sl1 WYIF, P to 1 st before gap, P2tog (1 st from each side of gap), P1, turn. 1 st dec.
Rep Short Rows 3–4 until all heel sts are worked. 18 (20, 22) heel sts.
Break C3.

Gusset
Continuing where C1 and C2 left off and using C2, PU sts along selvage edges of heel flap and rejoin for working in the rnd as follows.

Gusset Setup Rnd (C2): M1L between instep and heel flap (to close gap that would otherwise appear); PU and K 16 (18, 18) sts along first edge of heel flap (see *Notes* regarding Picking Up Stitches), K18 (20, 22) heel sts, PU and K 16 (18, 18) sts along second edge of heel flap. M1L between heel flap and instep; work Rnd 4 of Making Waves pattern across instep. 80 (90, 96) sts.
This is BOR; rearrange sts or place removable M as preferred.

Rnd 1: K1, SSK, K to last 3 sole sts, K2tog, K1, work across instep in pattern as established. 2 sts dec.
Rnd 2: K to end of sole sts, work across instep in pattern.
Rep Rnds 1–2 another 11 (12, 11) times. 56 (64, 72) sts.

Foot
WE as established, with sole in St st and instep in pattern, until sock measures 1.25 (1.5, 1.75)" shorter than desired total foot length from back of heel and ending on Rnd 3 or Rnd 7 of stitch pattern. Break C1 and C2.

Toe
Join C3. If desired foot length has not been met by ending on Rnd 3 or Rnd 7 of stitch pattern, extra Setup Rnds can be worked to achieve desired length.
Setup Rnd: K all.
Rnd 1: K1, SSK, K to 3 sts before instep, K2tog, K1; K1, SSK, K to last 3 sts, K2tog, K1. 4 sts dec.
Rnd 2: K all.
Rep Rnds 1–2 another 4 (5, 6) times. 36 (40, 44) sts.
Rep Rnd 1 another 4 (4, 5) times. 20 (24, 24) sts.

Left Sock
Work as right sock except use Making Waves Left pattern.

Finishing
Arrange sts so first 10 (12, 12) sts are on one needle and last 10 (12, 12) sts are on another needle. Graft toe sts closed.
Weave in ends, wash, and block as desired.

Making Waves Right

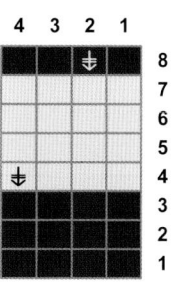

Making Waves Left

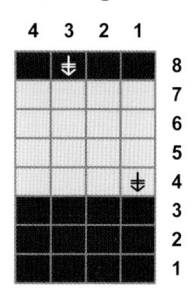

LEGEND

■ Contrasting Color 1

▨ Contrasting Color 2

☐ Knit Stitch

Dip Stitch (Dip)
Insert RH needle into front of third st below next st on LH needle, and draw up loop; then K next st on LH needle and pass loop over st just knitted

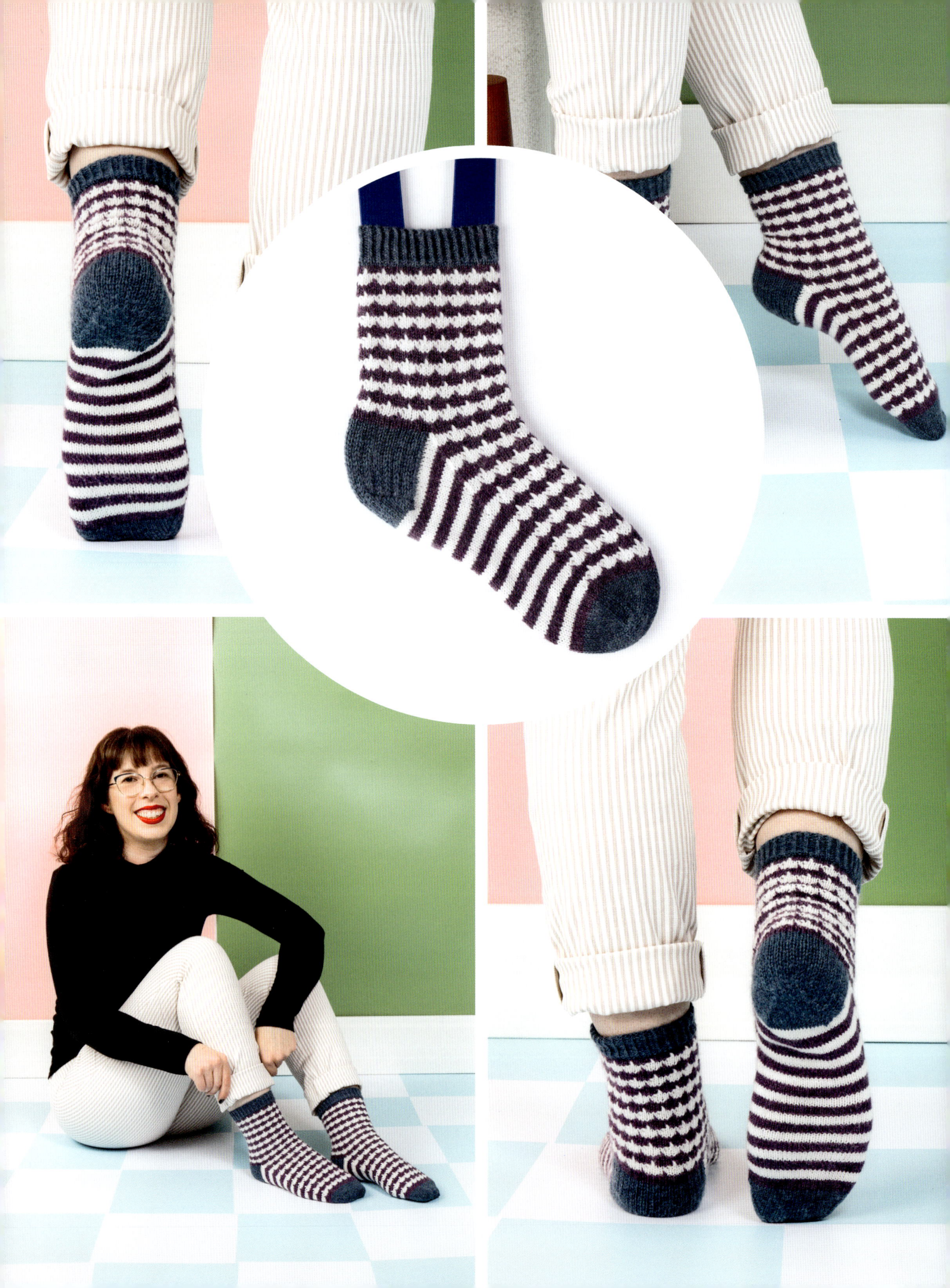

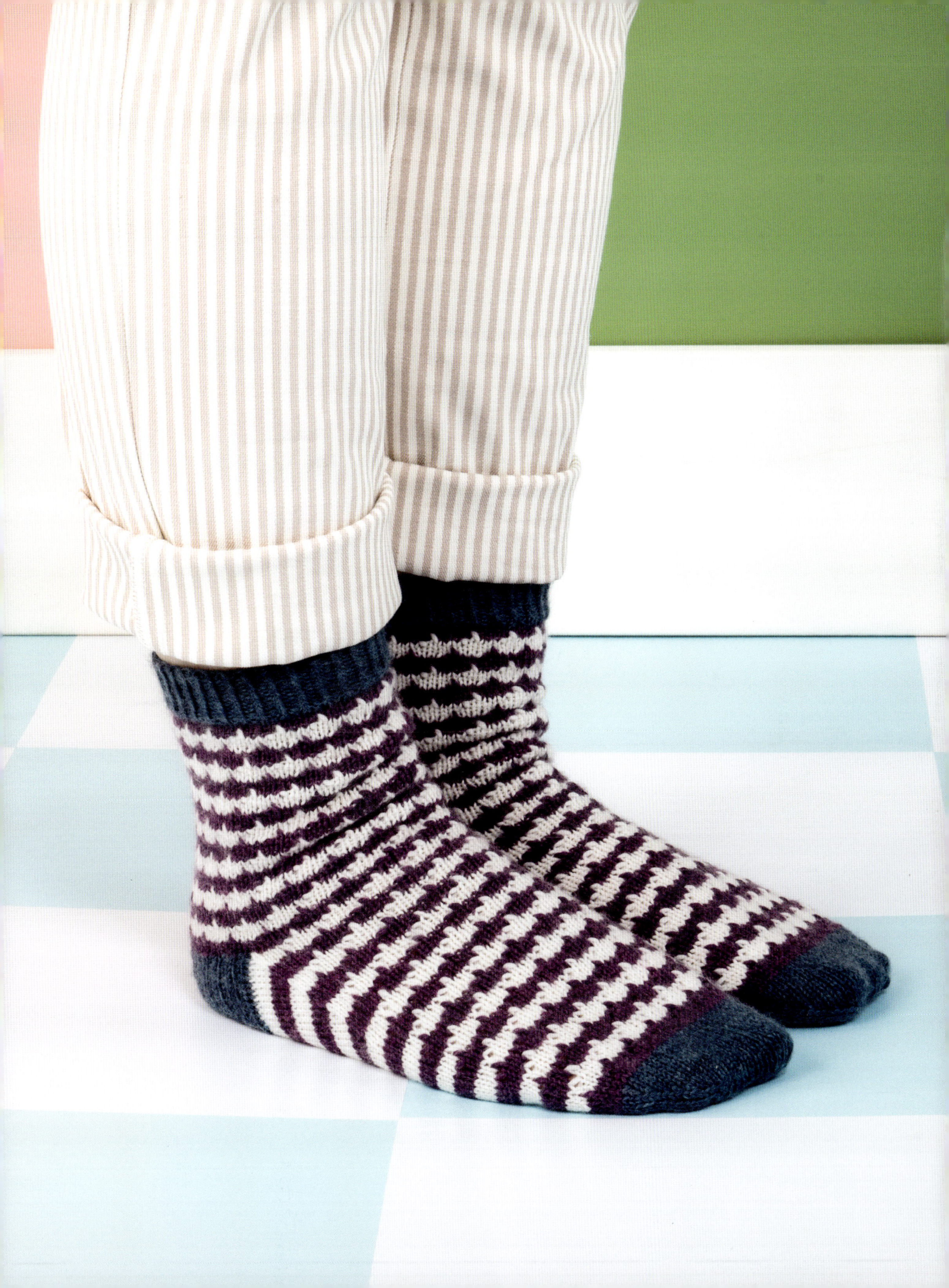

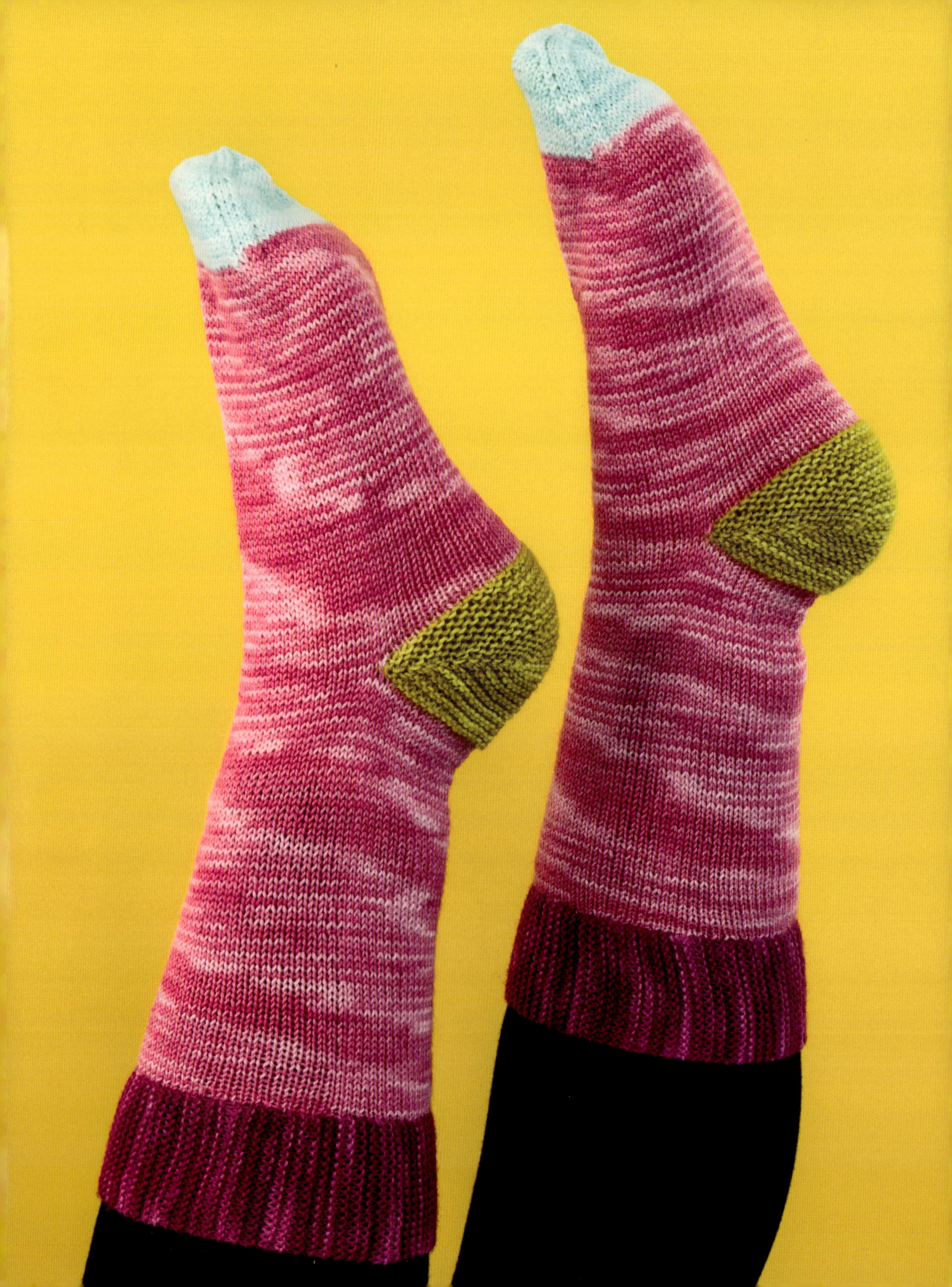

NO PURL SOCKS
by Holli Yeoh

FINISHED MEASUREMENTS
3.75 (4.75, 5.75, 6.5, 7.5)(8.5, 9.5, 10.25, 11.25)" foot and leg circumference × 4.25 (5.25, 6.5, 7, 8.25)(9.5, 10.5, 11.5, 12.75)" foot length; meant to be worn with approx 10% negative ease—choose a finished size approx 0.5" (smallest sizes) to 1.25" (largest sizes) smaller than foot circumference

YARN
Hawthorne™ (fingering weight, 80% Fine Superwash Highland Wool, 20% Polyamide (Nylon); 357 yards/100g): MC Camellia Kettle 28619, 1 (1, 1, 1, 1) (1, 1, 1, 2) hank(s); C1 Turkish Delight Kettle 26691, C2 Cattail Kettle 28620, C3 Nymph Kettle 28624, 1 hank each

NEEDLES
US 1 (2.25mm) DPNs or two circular needles for two circulars technique or 32" or longer circular needles for Magic Loop technique, or size to obtain gauge US 0 (2mm) two DPNs, straight or circular needles, or one size smaller than size used to obtain gauge

NOTIONS
Yarn Needle
Stitch Markers

GAUGE
34 sts and 50 rnds = 4" in Stockinette Stitch in the round, blocked

For pattern support, contact info@holliyeoh.com

No Purl Socks

Notes:
One plain, no purl! These socks make a virtue out of avoiding the knit stitch's less loved twin, leveraging garter stitch for elasticity and textural variation while providing a deeply relaxing project. Juicy colors with a zingy accent ensure that plain isn't boring.

The socks are worked cuff down, starting with a long strip of Garter Stitch grafted closed to create a ring. Stitches are then picked up and worked down in Stockinette Stitch for the leg and foot. The Garter Stitch short-row heel creates a cushy fabric and good fit. Finally, the wedge toe cinches it all shut. Sized from toddler to large adult.

Socks fit best with negative ease. As noted in the sizing info, choose a finished size that's 10–15% smaller than measured foot circumference (approx 0.5" (smallest sizes) to 1.25" (largest sizes) smaller). For the best fit in sock length, finished sock length should be shorter than measured foot length: about 0.25" shorter for feet less than 7" long and 0.5" shorter for feet more than 7" long. This negative ease in sock foot length is included in the instructions and it's not necessary to calculate it, unless you're modifying the pattern.

Short rows are worked using the Wrap & Turn technique. Because the heel is worked in Garter Stitch, it's not necessary to pick up and hide the wraps. Feel free to substitute a preferred short row turn method.

How to Identify Single- and Double-Wrapped Stitches
At the base of the st of a normal Garter Stitch st, there should be a purl bump, like a necklace around the st. Single-wrapped sts have two necklaces—the purl bump plus the wrap. Double-wrapped sts have three necklaces—the purl bump plus two wraps.

Grafting Garter Stitch
Setup sts on needles: Remove provisional CO, being sure to catch final loop (which isn't a true st) and place on needle, thus making the st count at each end of Garter Stitch cuff the same.
Hold needles parallel to one another with CO needle in front and needle with 14" tail in back, WSs tog. When viewed from RS, front needle has Garter Stitch ridge immediately below needle with P bumps appearing at base of sts on needle. Back needle, when viewed from WS, looks the same as front needle from RS.
Thread tail on needle.
Step 1: Insert threaded needle K-wise into first st on front needle, drop st off needle and pull yarn through.
Step 2: Insert needle behind yarn running from back needle to front needle, then P-wise into next st on front needle, leave st on needle, pull yarn through.
Step 3: Insert needle K-wise into next st on back needle, drop st off needle and pull yarn through.
Step 4: Insert needle P-wise into next st on back needle, leave st on needle, pull yarn through.
Step 5: Insert needle K-wise into next st on front needle, drop st off needle and pull yarn through.
Step 6: Insert needle P-wise into next st on front needle, leave st on needle, pull yarn through.
Rep Steps 3–6 until 1 st remains on each needle.
Work Step 3, then Step 5 once more.

DIRECTIONS

Garter Stitch Cuff
Using a provisional CO method and with C1 and smaller needles, CO 9 (13, 15, 15, 17)(17, 17, 17, 17) sts.
Work Garter Stitch for 63 (79, 95, 111, 127)(143, 159, 175, 191) rows—31 (39, 47, 55, 63)(71, 79, 87, 95) Garter Stitch ridges plus one more row—ending with a WS row.
Break yarn leaving a 14" tail for grafting.

Remove provisional CO and place sts on spare needle. Graft final row to first row to create a closed ring.

Leg
With MC and larger needles, PU and K 1 st in each Garter Stitch ridge along one edge of cuff. 32 (40, 48, 56, 64)(72, 80, 88, 96) sts. PM for BOR.
Distribute sts on needle(s) as follows.
For set of four DPNs: 16 (20, 24, 28, 32)(36, 40, 44, 48) sts on needle 1; 8 (10, 12, 14, 16)(18, 20, 22, 24) sts each on needles 2 and 3.
For set of five DPNs: 8 (10, 12, 14, 16)(18, 20, 22, 24) sts each on four needles.
For two circulars or Magic Loop: 16 (20, 24, 28, 32)(36, 40, 44, 48) sts each on needle and cable.

Work St st (K all rnds) until piece measures 2.5 (4.5, 6.25, 7, 7)(8, 8, 8.5, 8.5)" including cuff, ending at BOR. Do not break yarn.

Garter Stitch Heel
Heel Decreases
Row 1 (RS): With C2, K5 (7, 8, 9, 11)(12, 13, 15, 16), PM, K6 (6, 8, 10, 10)(12, 14, 14, 16), PM, K4 (6, 7, 8, 10)(11, 12, 14, 15), W&T. Short rows will be worked on each side of center 6 (6, 8, 10, 10)(12, 14, 14, 16) sts indicated by Ms.
Row 2 (WS): K14 (18, 22, 26, 30)(34, 38, 42, 46), W&T.
Row 3: K to 1 st before wrapped st, W&T.
Rep Row 3 every row until all heel sts to outside of marked center sts have been wrapped, ending with a WS row. 6 (6, 8, 10, 10)(12, 14, 14, 16) unwrapped sts in center. There should be an equal number of wrapped sts on each side.

Heel Increases
See note about single- and double-wrapped sts.
Row 1 (RS): K to first wrapped st, K1, W&T. Newly wrapped st now has two wraps.
Row 2 (WS): Rep Row 1.
Row 3: K to next double-wrapped st, K1, W&T.

Rep Row 3 every row until all heels sts outside of marked center sts have been worked and no single-wrapped sts remain, ending with a WS row. There's 1 remaining double-wrapped st at beginning and end of heel row. Heel Ms may be removed on next rnd.

Foot
Resume MC, with RS facing, work St st in the rnd until foot measures 3.5 (4.25, 5.25, 5.5, 6.5)(7.5, 8.25, 9, 10)" from back of heel, or 1 (1.25, 1.5, 2, 2.25)(2.5, 2.75, 3, 3.25)" shorter than measured foot length, ending at BOR. Break yarn.

Toe
Dec Rnd: With C3, (K1, SSK, K to 3 sts before M, K2tog, K1) two times. 4 sts dec.
Knit one rnd.
Rep Dec Rnd every other rnd 2 (3, 4, 5, 6)(7, 8, 9, 10) more times. 20 (24, 28, 32, 36)(40, 44, 48, 52) sts.
Rep Dec Rnd every rnd 3 (4, 5, 6, 7)(8, 9, 10, 11) times. 8 sts. Break yarn, thread tail through remaining sts, pull tight and fasten securely.

Second Sock
Make second sock same as first.

Finishing
Weave in ends, wash, and block as desired.

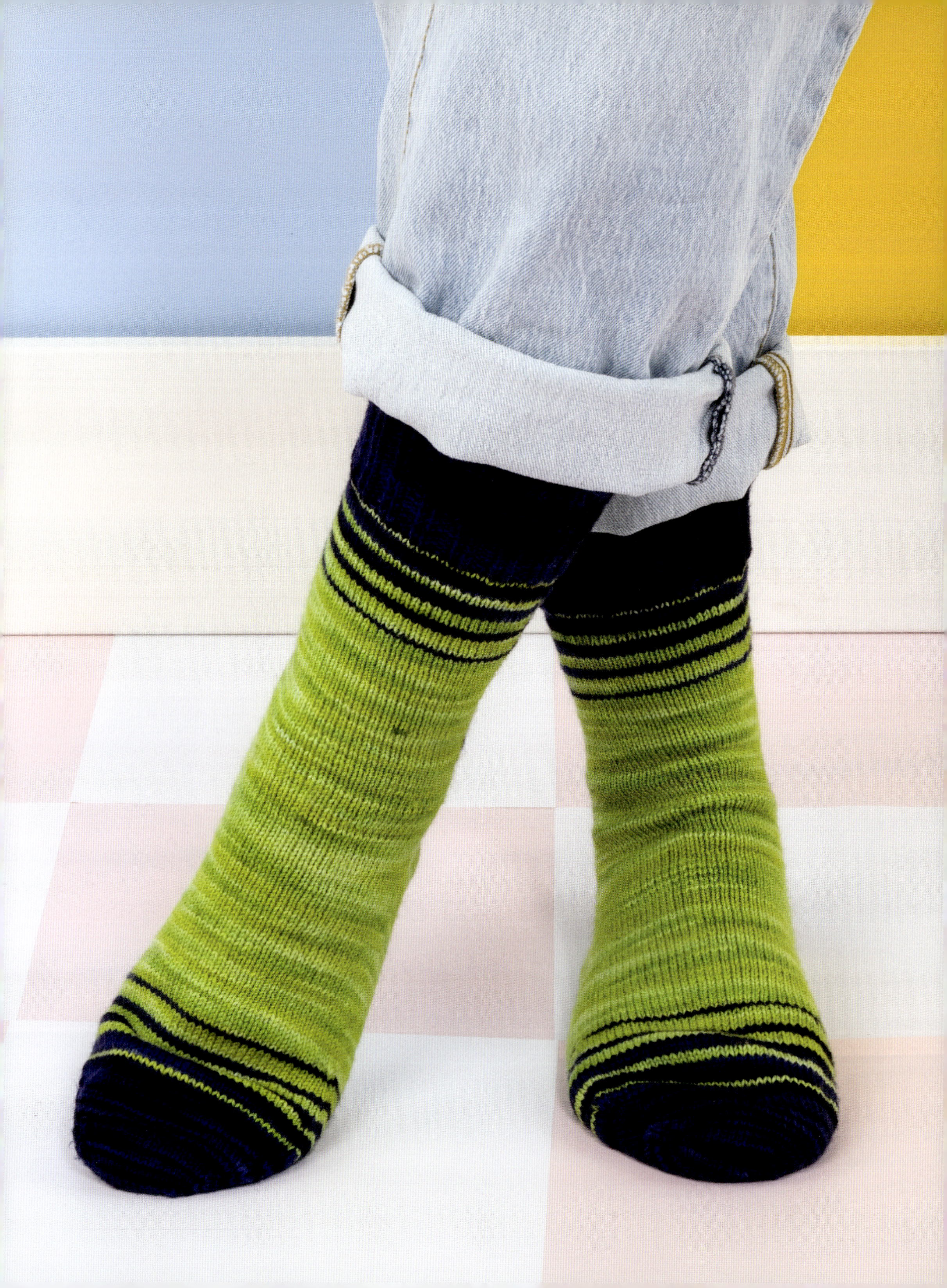

PINNER SOCKS
by Jo Torr

FINISHED MEASUREMENTS
6.25 (7, 8, 9)" foot circumference × variable foot length; meant to be worn with approx 10% negative ease; 6" leg length, measured from top of heel flap, adjustable (includes 2" cuff)

YARN
Stroll™ Tonal (fingering weight, 75% Fine Superwash Merino Wool, 25% Nylon; 462 yards/100g); MC Kiwi 28264, CC Orbit 27060, 1 skein each

NEEDLES
US 1 (2.25mm) DPNs or two circular needles for two circulars technique or 32" or longer circular needles for Magic Loop technique, or size to obtain gauge

NOTIONS
Yarn Needle
Stitch Markers

GAUGE
36 sts and 44 rnds = 4" in Stockinette Stitch in the round, blocked

For pattern support, contact support@jotorr.co.uk

Pinner Socks

Notes:
Make these socks shine by using two contrasting colors in a simple but effective striped pattern that moves between one color and the next with a pleasing sense of ebb and flow.

These socks are knit toe-up with an integrated gusset and heel flap. Both the heel flap and under the heel are reinforced for extra durability. Instructions are provided to avoid a jog when changing colors.

Slip all stitches purl-wise, with yarn held to the back.

All sizes as written account for 0.25" negative ease for a snug fit.

Jog
To avoid a noticeable jog at the BOR when changing colors, work the first rnd in new color, then pick up first stitch of final rnd in previous color and place it on LH needle. Knit together with first stitch of next rnd.

M-A/B/C = Stitch Markers A/B/C

Where to Start Gusset
Instructions are given for the pattern gauge. If row gauge is different from pattern gauge, then divide 42 (48, 54, 60) by number of rows per 1". Subtract this from actual foot length, then subtract 0.25" more to allow for negative ease. This is the measurement to knit to before beginning gusset increases.

DIRECTIONS

Toe
Using Judy's Magic Cast On and CC, CO 20 (20, 28, 32) sts and distribute evenly across needles; PM for BOR.
Setup Rnd: K10 (10, 14, 16), PM-A, K to end.
Rnd 1: (KFB, K to 2 sts before M, KFB, K1, SM) two times. 4 sts inc.
Rnd 2: K all.
Rep Rnds 1-2 another 7 (9, 9, 10) times.
Rep Rnd 1 once more. 56 (64, 72, 80) sts.

Foot
First 28 (32, 36, 40) sts are instep, second 28 (32, 36, 40) sts are sole.
Rnd 1: Join MC and K all.
Rnd 2: With CC, K all.
Rnd 3: Jog (see *Notes*), K to end.
Rnds 4-5: K all.
Rnd 6: With MC, K all.
Rnd 7: Jog, K to end.
Rnd 8: With CC, K all.
Rnd 9: Rep Rnd 3.
Rnd 10: K all.
Rnd 11: With MC, K all.
Rnd 12: Rep Rnd 7.
Rnd 13: K all.
Rnd 14: With CC, K all.
Rnd 15: Rep Rnd 3.
Rnd 16: With MC, K all.
Rnd 17: Rep Rnd 7.
Rnds 18-19: K all.
Rnd 20: With CC, K all. Break CC.
Rnd 21: With MC, K all.
Rnd 22: Rep Rnd 7.
With MC, work until sock is 4 (4.5, 5.25, 5.75)" shorter than desired foot length. (See *Notes* if row gauge does not match pattern gauge).

Gusset Increases
Rnd 1: K to M-A, SM, K1, PM-B, M1R, K to last st, M1L, PM-C, K1. 2 sts inc.
Rnd 2: K all.
New Ms separate gusset sts on each side from central 28 (32, 36, 40) sole sts.
Rnd 3: K to M-A, SM, K1, M1R, K to M-B, SM, K to M-C, SM, K to last st, M1L, K1. 2 sts inc.
Rnd 4: K all.
Rep Rnds 3-4 another 11 (13, 15, 17) times.
Rep Rnd 3 once more.

Next Rnd: (K to M, SM) three times, K1 (3, 3, 3), (M1L, K2) 6 (6, 7, 8) times, K1.
Next Rnd: K to M-A, SM, K2, join CC, do not break MC; with CC, K1, M1R, (K2, M1R) 5 (5, 6, 7) times, K1 (3, 3, 3), SM-B. 20 (22, 25, 28) gusset sts each side.

Heel Turn
Heel turn begins at M-B. Work back and forth on sole sts between M-B and M-C.
Short Row 1 (RS): With CC, K to 2 sts before M-C, W&T.
Short Row 2 (WS): P to 2 sts before M-B, W&T.
Short Row 3: K1, (Sl1, K1) to 1 st before previous turn, W&T.
Short Row 4: P to 1 st before previous turn, W&T.
Short Row 5: K1, (K1, Sl1) to 1 st before previous turn, W&T.
Short Row 6: Rep Short Row 4.
Rep Short Rows 3-6 another 2 (3, 3, 4) times.
Rep Short Rows 3-4 another 0 (0, 1, 1) times. 8 (10, 11, 13) sts each side, 7 (9, 10, 12) sts wrapped, 12 (12, 14, 14) center sts.

Next Short Row (RS): Work as established to first wrap, K6 (8, 9, 11) (working wraps tog with sts), SSK (working wrap tog with st). 27 (31, 35, 39) sole sts.
Next Short Row (WS): Sl1, P to first wrap, P6 (8, 9, 11) (working wraps tog with sts), P2tog (working wrap tog with st). 26 (30, 34, 38) sole sts.

Heel Flap
Cont working back and forth.
Short Row 1 (RS): With CC, Sl1 (K1, Sl1) to 1 st before M-C; remove M, SSK, turn.
Short Row 2 (WS): Sl1, P to 1 st before M-B; remove M, P2tog, turn.
Short Row 3: Sl1 (K1, Sl1) to 1 st before gap, SSK, turn.
Short Row 4: Sl1, P to 1 st before gap, P2tog, turn.

Rep Short Rows 3–4 until 2 sts remain outside each gap. 58 (66, 74, 82) sts.
Break CC.
Next Row (RS): With MC, K across heel flap to 1 st before gap, SSK, K1. 57 (65, 73, 81) sts.

Leg
Return to working in the rnd.

Solid Section
Rnd 1: With MC, K to M-A, SM, K1, K2tog, K to end. 56 (64, 72, 80) sts.
Rnd 2: K all.
Rep Rnd 2 until leg measures 2″ from top of heel flap, or 4″ shorter than desired length.

Striped Section
Rnd 1: Join CC and K all.
Rnd 2: With MC, K all.
Rnd 3: Jog, K to end.
Rnds 4–5: K all.
Rnd 6: With CC, K all.
Rnd 7: Jog, K to end.
Rnd 8: With MC, K all.
Rnd 9: Rep Rnd 3.
Rnd 10: K all.
Rnd 11: With CC, K all.
Rnd 12: Rep Rnd 7.
Rnd 13: K all.
Rnd 14: With MC, K all.
Rnd 15: Rep Rnd 3.
Rnd 16: With CC, K all.
Rnd 17: Rep Rnd 7.
Rnds 18–19: K all.
Rnd 20: With MC, K all.
Break MC.
Rnd 21: With CC, K all.
Rnd 22: Jog, K to end.

Cuff
Rnd 1: With CC, (K2 TBL, P2) to end.
Rep Rnd 1 until cuff measures 2″ or desired length.
BO using Jeny's Surprisingly Stretchy Bind Off.

Second Sock
Make second sock same as first.

Finishing
Weave in ends, wash, and block as desired.

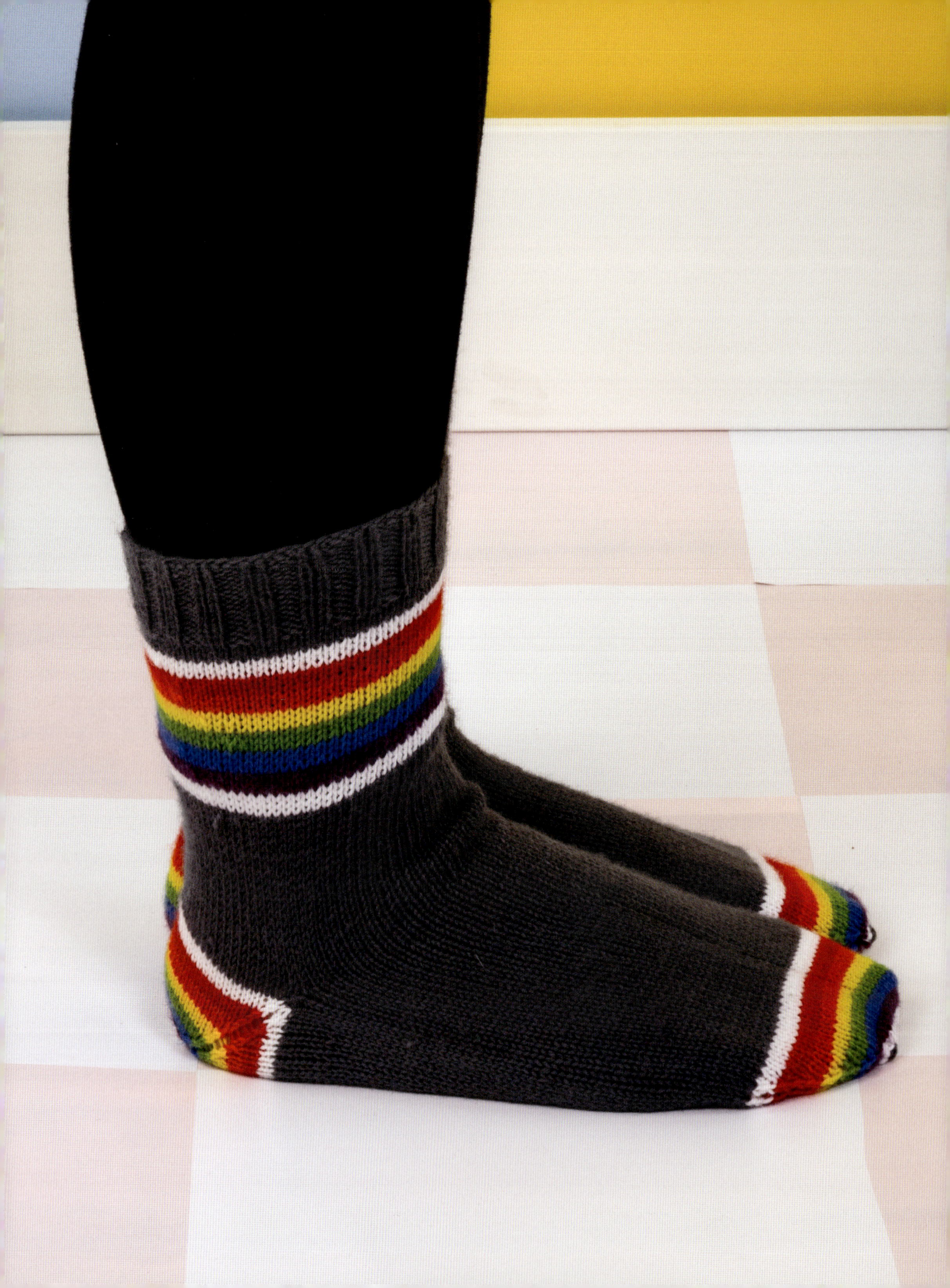

RAINBOW SOCKS
by Allison Griffith

FINISHED MEASUREMENTS
7 (7.5, 8, 8.5, 9, 9.5)" leg circumference × 9 (9, 10, 10, 11, 11)" foot length; meant to be worn with zero or slight negative ease

YARN
Stroll™ (fingering weight, 75% Fine Superwash Merino Wool, 25% Nylon; 231 yards/50g): MC Ash 23696, 2 skeins
and
Stroll™ Mini Pack (fingering weight, 75% Fine Superwash Merino Wool, 25% Nylon 644 yards/140g total; 92 yards/20g per mini-hank): Rainbow 29875, 1 pack (C1 White 26082, C2 Strawberry 28179, C3 Buoy 28180, C4 Dandelion 25024, C5 Peapod 25026, C6 Rhapsody 28185, C7 Duchess Heather 24594)

NEEDLES
US 1 (2.25mm) set of five DPNs, or size to obtain gauge

NOTIONS
Yarn Needle
Stitch Marker (a split marker or safety pin is recommended)
Scrap Yarn

GAUGE
34 sts and 50 rnds = 4" in Stockinette Stitch in the round, blocked

For pattern support, contact knittingontheneedles@gmail.com

Rainbow Socks

Notes:
These cheerful socks are just the ticket for using up the small amounts of special, bright yarn that's been hanging out in your stash (or a favorite pack of mini-skeins!). They are a labor of love, but totally worth it. They're sure to be a favorite for years to come!

Rainbow Socks are worked in the rnd from the top down. Ribbing is worked at the cuff, followed by a series of stripes (weaving in ends as you go). Waste yarn is added for an afterthought heel. The heel and toe are both worked in the same way (decreasing at either side while working stripes at the same time). The toe and heel are closed with grafting and remaining ends are woven in.

To save time later, weave in ends as you go throughout all the striped sections.

DIRECTIONS

Cuff
With MC, loosely CO 60 (64, 68, 72, 76, 80) sts. Divide sts evenly between four DPNs. PM for BOR (a split-ring marker or safety pin works best for this) and prepare to work in the rnd, being careful not to twist sts.
Work 2x2 Rib for 1.5".

Leg
Knit three rnds. Break MC.
Join C1, knit three rnds, break yarn.
Join C2, knit three rnds, break yarn.
Join C3, knit three rnds, break yarn.
Join C4, knit three rnds, break yarn.
Join C5, knit three rnds, break yarn.
Join C6, knit three rnds, break yarn.
Join C7, knit three rnds, break yarn.
Join C1, knit three rnds, break yarn.
Join MC and knit until sock leg measures 6" from CO edge, or desired length.

Setup for Afterthought Heel
K45 (48, 51, 54, 57, 60); set aside MC but do not break; with contrasting scrap yarn, K30 (32, 34, 36, 38, 40), break scrap yarn; pick up MC yarn from where you left it, and K across scrap yarn sts, K to end.

Foot
WE in St st until foot measures approx 5.75 (5.5, 6.25, 5.75, 6.5, 6.25)" from scrap yarn, or 3.25 (3.5, 3.75, 4.25, 4.5, 4.75)" shorter than desired foot length, ending at BOR M. Break yarn.

Toe
Double-check that the 60 (64, 68, 72, 76, 80) sts are evenly distributed across four needles, 15 (16, 17, 18, 19, 20) sts on each needle. Needles 1 and 4 are on sole (heel side) of sock, Needles 2 and 3 are on top of sock.

Read the following instructions through before beginning toe. Work the following Stripe Sequence, breaking yarn with every color change, while at the same time working Dec Rnds 1–2 until 20 sts remain. Not all stripes will be worked for smaller sizes.

Stripe Sequence
Rnds 1–3: C1.
Rnds 4–6: C2.
Rnds 7–9: C3.
Rnds 10–12: C4.
Rnds 13–15: C5.
Rnds 16–18: C6.
Rnds 19–21: C7.
Rnds 22–24: C1.
Rnds 25–end: MC.

Dec Rnd 1: Needle 1—K to last 2 sts, K2tog; Needle 2—SSK, K to end; Needle 3—K to last 2 sts, K2tog; Needle 4—SSK, K to end. 4 sts dec.
Dec Rnd 2: K all.
Work Dec Rnds 1–2 another 8 (9, 10, 11, 12, 13) times, then rep Rnd 1 once more. 20 sts.

End: K5; break yarn, leaving a long (18" or longer) tail. Consolidate sts so the 10 sts on top of foot and the 10 sts on bottom of foot are on separate needles.

Graft toe sts closed.

Afterthought Heel
Carefully remove scrap yarn and PU the 60 (64, 68, 72, 76, 80) live sts around heel opening. Divide sts evenly across four needles; 15 (16, 17, 18, 19, 20) sts on each needle. Be sure that two needles lie at bottom of foot (Needles 1 and 4) and two needles lie across back of heel (Needles 2 and 3).
Begin at center bottom of foot with C1 and work Afterthought Heel in the same way as Toe.

Second Sock
Make second sock same as first.

Finishing
Weave in remaining ends, wash, and block as desired.

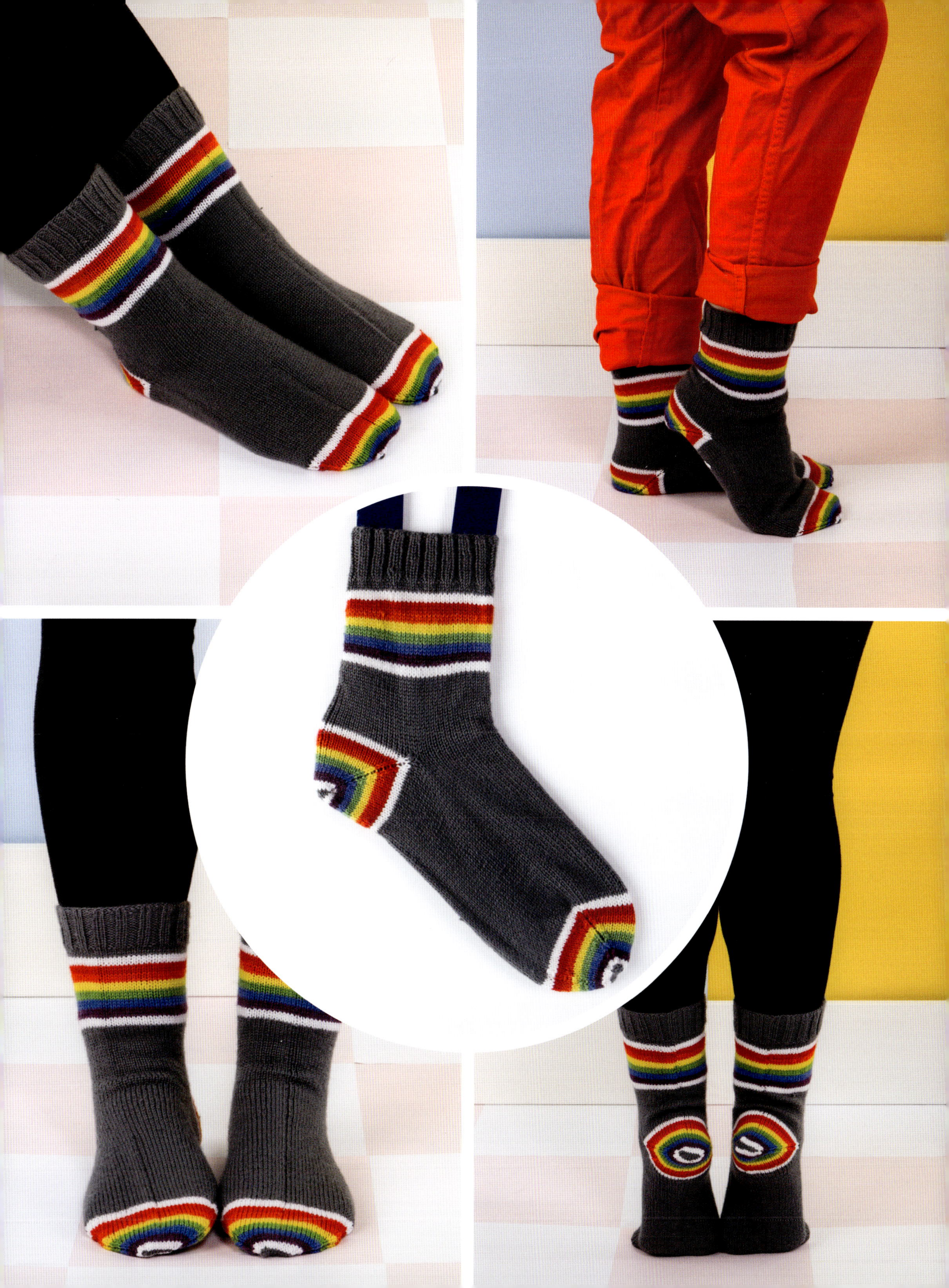

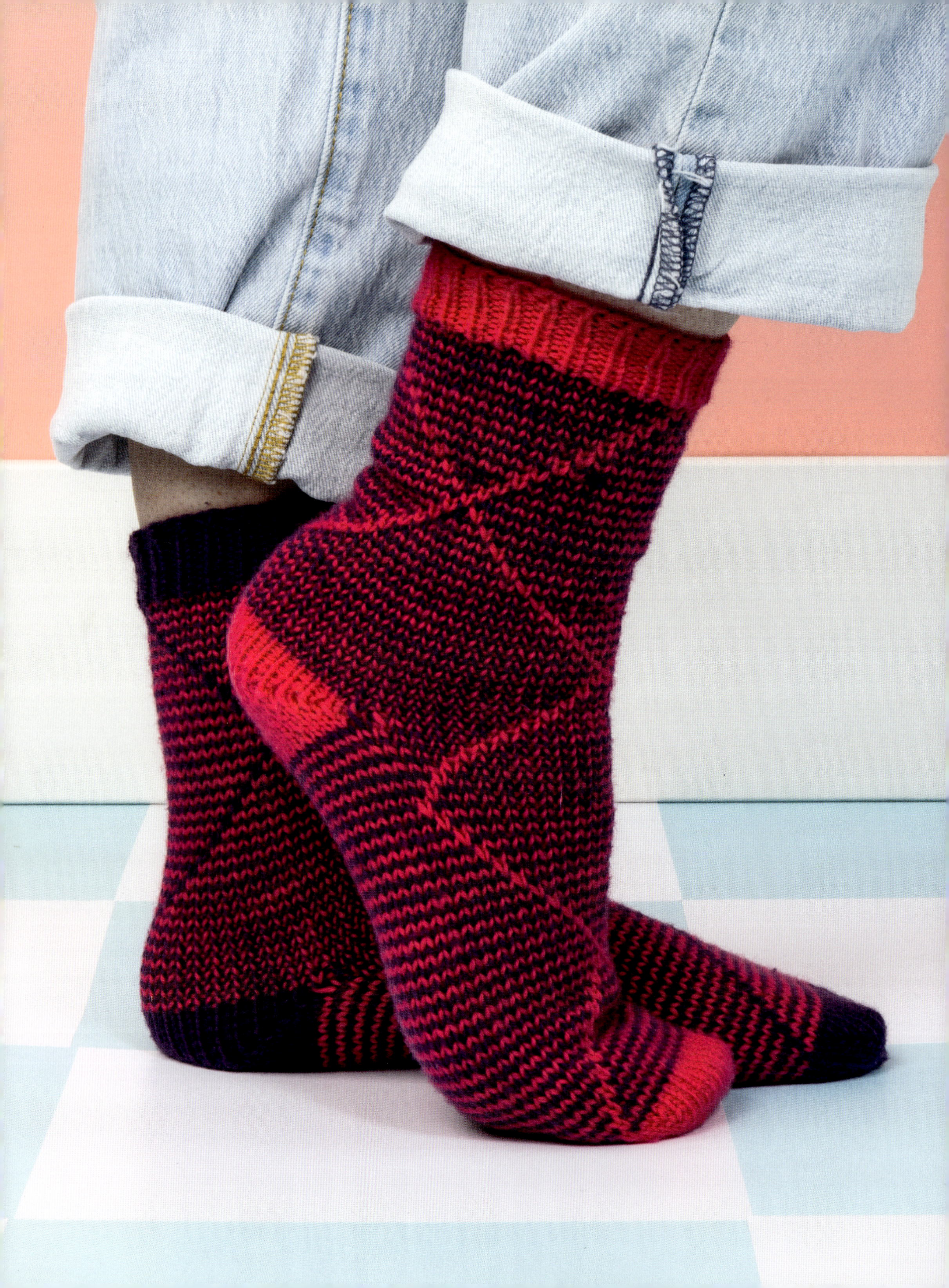

REBOUND SOCKS
by Lauren Rose

FINISHED MEASUREMENTS
7.25 (8, 9.25, 10)" leg circumference × 8.75 (9.25, 9.5, 10)" foot length (length is adjustable); meant to be worn with approx 10% negative ease, to fit US shoe sizes 6.5-7 (7.5-8, 8.5-9, 9.5-10)

YARN
Swish™ (DK weight, 100% Fine Superwash Merino Wool; 123 yards/50g): Crush 28640, Eggplant 24049, 1 (1, 2, 2) skeins each
Yardage is calculated based on a fraternal pair; if using same MC for both socks, more of that color might be needed

NEEDLES
US 3 (3.25mm) DPNs or two circular needles for two circulars technique or 32" or longer circular needles for Magic Loop technique, or size to obtain gauge

NOTIONS
Yarn Needle
Stitch Markers

GAUGE
24 sts and 38 rnds = 4" in Stockinette Stitch in the round, blocked

For pattern support, contact laurooftheblings@gmail.com

Rebound Socks   45

Rebound Socks

Notes:
Stripes and an intuitive slip-stitch pattern in this DK-weight sock make for relaxing knitting and a quick finished object. Swap colors on the second sock for a fraternal pair!

Moving slipped stitches on this striped sock create a diamond design on the foot and leg. Work the optional mini-gusset for a deeper heel, and the calf shaping for more room in the leg.

Short row instructions are written using the Shadow Wraps method, but can be substituted with another favorite wrapping technique.

KSW (Knit Shadow Wrap)
Lift right leg st directly below next st onto LH needle and knit, move st just knit to LH needle with its twin.

KDSW (Knit Double Shadow Wrap)
Work a second shadow wrap onto a KSW st.

PSW (Purl Shadow Wrap)
Slip next st to RH needle and lift left leg of st directly below it onto LH needle, purl this st, then slip new st and its twin back to LH needle as one.

PDSW (Purl Double Shadow Wrap)
Work a second shadow wrap onto a PSW st.

DIRECTIONS

Toe
With MC and using Judy's Magic Cast On or favorite toe-up cast on, CO 7 (7, 9, 9) sts across two needles. 14 (14, 18, 18) sts total.
PM for BOR. First 7 (7, 9, 9) sts are instep, second 7 (7, 9, 9) sts are sole.
Knit one rnd.
Inc Rnd: On instep, K1, KFB, K to last 3 sts of instep, KFB, K2; rep across sole. 4 sts inc.
Rep Inc Rnd 3 (3, 5, 5) more times. 15 (15, 21, 21) sts on instep and sole; 30 (30, 42, 42) sts total.

Rnd 1: K all.
Rnd 2: Work Inc Rnd.
Rep Rnds 1–2 another 2 (3, 2, 3) times. 21 (23, 27, 29) sts on instep and sole; 42 (46, 54, 58) sts total.
Next Rnd: K all.
Next Rnd: Work Inc Rnd across instep sts ONLY, knitting all sole sts. 2 sts inc on instep; 44 (48, 56, 60) sts total.
Knit one more rnd.

Foot
Join CC.

First Section
Rnd 1 (CC): Sl1, K to 1 st before end of instep, Sl1, K to end.
Rnd 2 (MC): K all.
Rnd 3 (CC): K to first Sl st, K1 (the Sl st), Sl1, K to 1 st before second Sl st, Sl1, K to end.
(*Note:* The Sl sts will look like 2 MC sts on top of each other.)

Rnd 4 (MC): K all.
Rep Rnds 3–4 until Sl sts meet in center of instep, ending with Rnd 4.
Final **Rnd 3 will be worked as follows:** K to first Sl st, K1, Sl1, K to end. (There will be only 1 Sl st between the 2 sts slipped on previous row).

Second Section
Rnd 1 (CC): K to 1 st before Sl st, Sl1, K1, Sl1, K to end.
Rnd 2 (MC): K all.
Rnd 3 (CC): K to 1 st before first Sl st, Sl1, K to second Sl st, K1, Sl1, K to end.
Rnd 4 (MC): K all.
Rep Rnds 3–4 until Sl sts reach end of instep (same as First Section Rnd 1), ending with Rnd 3.

Gusset
Move to Mini-Gusset and Heel according to measurements below, beginning either mini-gusset or heel on an MC rnd. The optional mini-gusset will add more depth to the heel and is suited for knitters with a high instep.

If Working Mini-Gusset
Rep First Section beginning with Rnd 2, working until foot measures 2.5 (3, 3.25, 3.5)" shorter than desired length; move to (Optional) Mini-Gusset Increases instructions.

If Working Heel Only
Rep First Section beginning with Rnd 2, working until foot measures 1.75 (2, 2, 2.25)" shorter than desired length; move to Heel Turn instructions.

(Optional) Mini-Gusset Increases
Setup (MC): Work instep in pattern as established; on sole, M1R, PM, K to end of sole, PM, M1L. 2 sts inc.
Rnd 1 (CC): Work instep as established; K all sole sts.
Rnd 2 (MC): Work instep as established; on sole, K to M, M1R, SM, K to M, SM, M1L, K to end of sole. 2 sts inc.
Rep Rnds 1–2 another 2 (3, 3, 4) times; 4 (5, 5, 6) sts on either side of Ms.
Rep Rnd 1 once more. 8 (10, 10, 12) sts inc on sole.

Heel Turn
Heel is worked in short rows using MC. If working mini-gusset, heel will be worked in between 2 st Ms placed on heel side.

Cont instep sts in pattern as established.
Mini-Gusset Only: K to M, SM.
Short Row 1 (RS): K20 (22, 26, 28), KSW, turn.
Short Row 2 (WS): P19 (21, 25, 27), PSW, turn.
Short Row 3: K to 1 st before wrapped st, KSW, turn.
Short Row 4: P to 1 st before wrapped st, PSW, turn.
Rep Short Rows 3–4 until there are 7 (9, 9, 11) unwrapped sts in center of heel, ending with Short Row 4. 7 (7, 9, 9) wrapped sts on either side.

Next Short Row (RS): K7 (9, 9, 11) unwrapped center sts to first wrapped st and K tog with its wrap; KDSW, turn.

Next Short Row (WS): P unwrapped sts to first wrapped st and P tog with its wrap; PDSW, turn.
Next Short Row: K unwrapped sts to double-wrapped st and K tog with its wraps; KDSW, turn.
Next Short Row: P unwrapped sts to double-wrapped st and P tog with its wraps; PDSW, turn.
Rep last two Short Rows until all heel sts have been worked, ending with a WS row. There will be one double-wrapped st at each end of heel.

Knit across heel, working wrapped st at end tog with its wraps.
Mini-Gusset Only: SM and K to end.
Do not turn.

If working mini-gusset, cont with Mini-Gusset Decreases. If not, work as follows: With CC, work instep as established; on back of leg, K wrapped st at beginning of heel sts tog with its wraps and K to end. Then, move to Leg instructions.

(Optional) Mini-Gusset Decreases
Setup Rnd (CC): Work instep as established; on back of leg, K to M, remove M, work wrapped st tog with its wraps, PM, K to 1 st before M, PM, K1, remove M, K to end. 5 (6, 6, 7) sts on either side of Ms.
Rnd 1 (MC): Work instep as established; on back of leg, K to 2 sts before M, K2tog, SM, K to M, SM, SSK, K to end. 2 sts dec.
Rnd 2 (CC): Work instep as established; K to end, slipping all Ms.
Rep Rnds 1–2 until there is only 1 st on either side of Ms. Remove Ms on subsequent rnd. 8 (10, 10, 12) sts dec; 21 (23, 27, 29) sts on back of leg.

Leg
Note: See end of pattern for optional calf-shaping.
Cont alternating between MC and CC and working pattern as established on instep.
Begin slip-stitch pattern on back of leg either on CC rnd where there is 1 Sl st in center of instep, or CC rnd with 2 Sl sts on either side of instep.

If single Sl st rnd
Rnd 1 (CC): Work instep as established (slipping center st); on back of leg, K10 (11, 13, 14), Sl1, K to end.
Rnd 2 (MC): K all.
There will be one CC rnd where instep has 2 Sl sts on either end, and back of leg has none. Work that part according to the four rnds below.

If 2 Sl sts on either side rnd
Rnd 1 (CC): Work instep as established (Sl1, K to 1 before end of instep, Sl1); K to end.
Rnd 2 (MC): K all.
Rnd 3 (CC): Work instep as established (K to first Sl st, Sl1, K to 1 before second Sl st, Sl1, K to end of instep); on back of leg, Sl1, K to last st, Sl1.
Rnd 4 (MC): K all.

Cont moving Sl sts as established.
Move to Cuff instructions after working CC rnd where there is 1 Sl st in center of instep or CC rnd with 2 Sl sts on either side of instep.

Cuff
Break CC.
With MC, knit one rnd.
Work 1x1 Rib for ten rnds.
With Jeny's Surprisingly Stretchy Bind Off or favorite stretchy bind off, BO all sts. Break MC.

Second Sock
Make second sock same as the first, switching MC and CC for a fraternal pair.

Finishing
Weave in ends, wash, and block as desired.

(Optional) Calf Shaping
Measure calf where cuff of sock will hit and subtract 1": ____

Multiply that number by 6 and round to nearest whole even number: ____
This is the target stitch count.

Take target stitch count and subtract stitch count of the size being knit on foot: ____

Divide that number by 2: ____
This is how many sts will be added on the leg.

Note: Begin working calf shaping after the rnd with 2 Sl sts on edges of instep (when Sl sts are moving towards center).

Rnd 1 (MC): Work instep as established; on back of leg, M1R, work as established to end, M1L. 2 sts inc.
Rnds 2–4: Work as established.
Rnd 5 (MC): M1R, work instep as established, M1L; work back of leg as established. 2 sts inc.
Rnds 6–8: Work as established.

If increasing 2 sts every fourth rnd would make leg too long, work incs as described every MC rnd, alternating between adding to sole and instep.

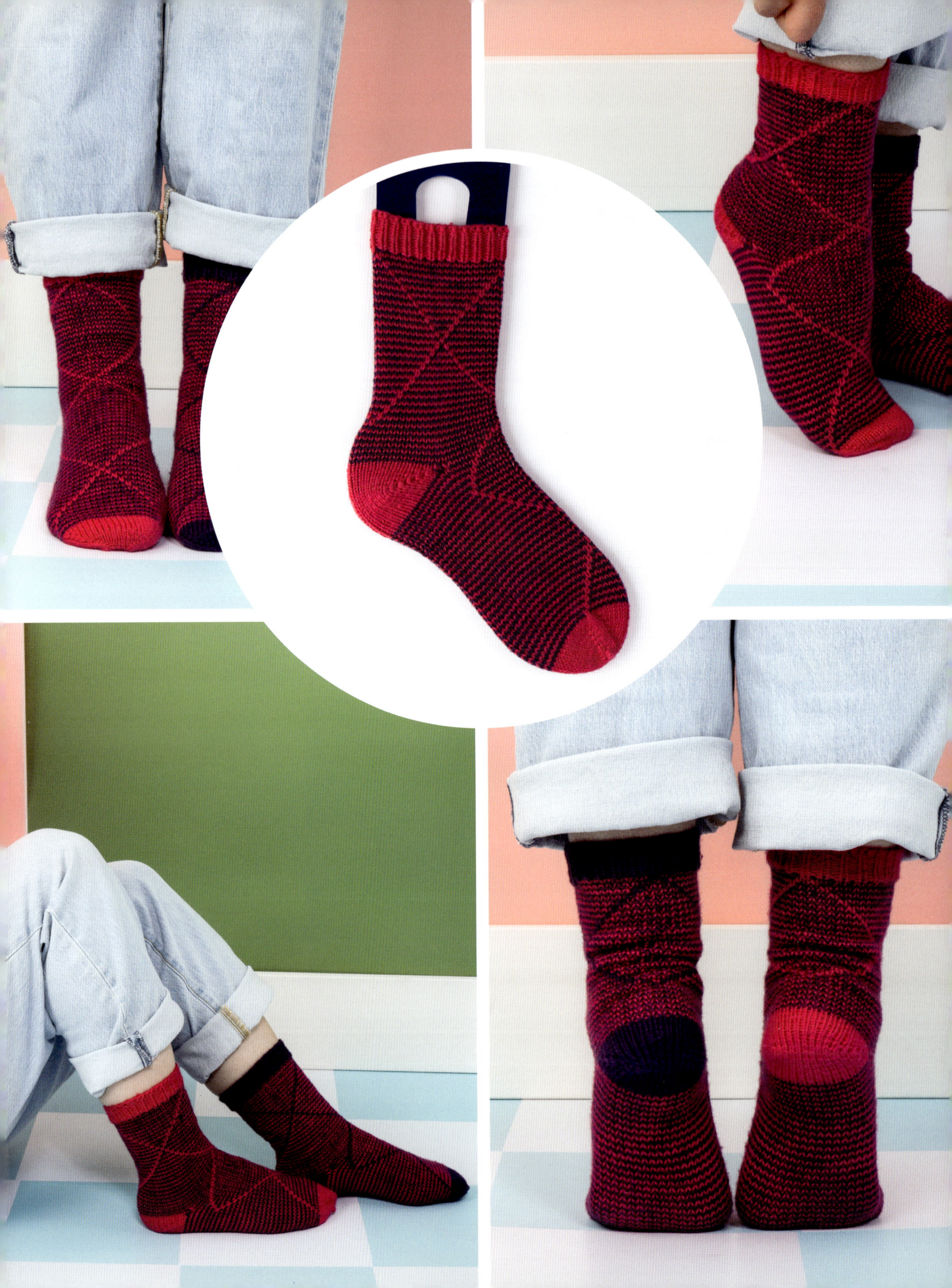

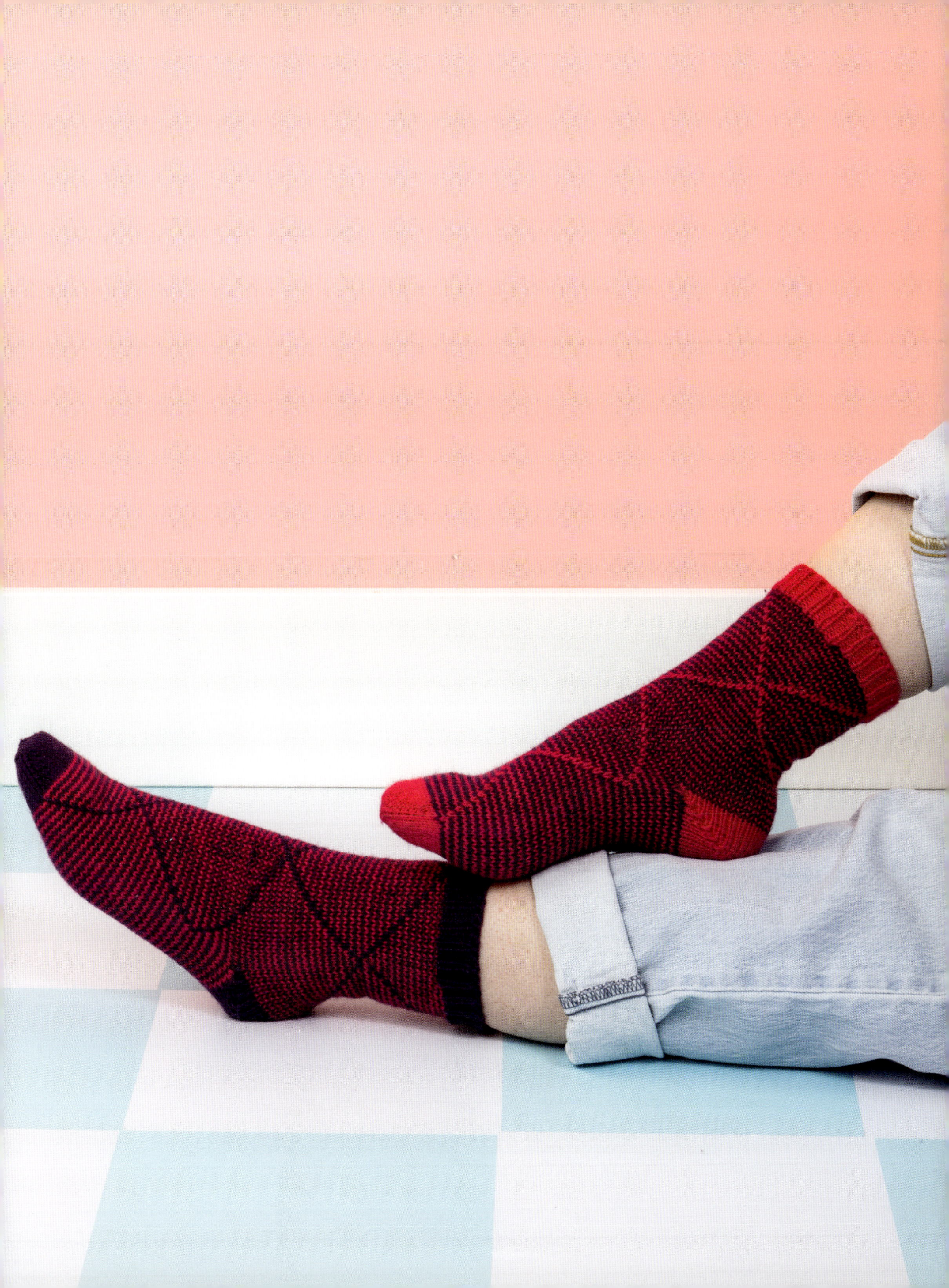

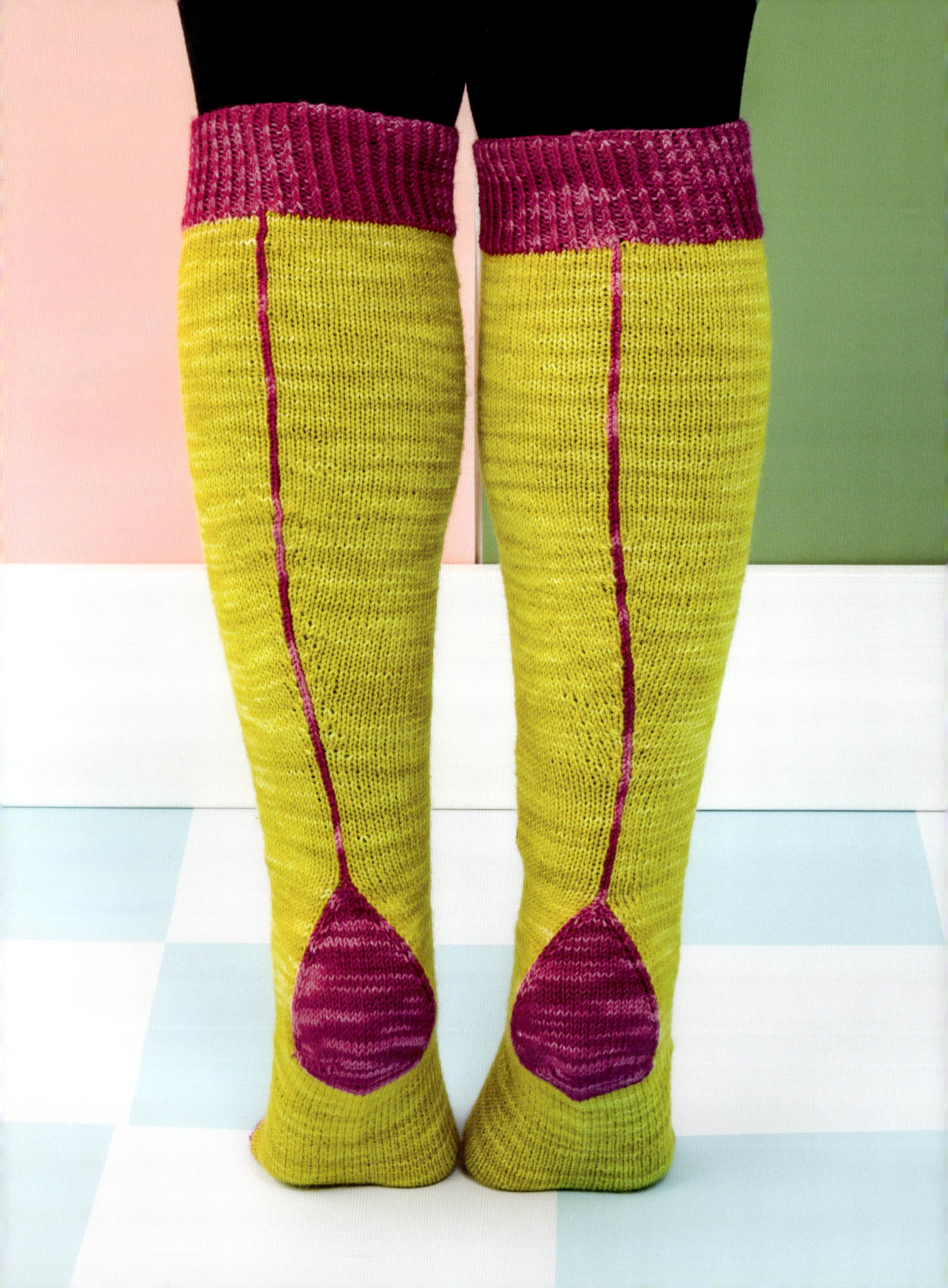

SEAMLESS SEAM SOCKS
by Mone Dräger

FINISHED MEASUREMENTS
9 (10.5, 12)" circumference at calf and 7 (8, 9)" circumference at ankle/foot × 15 (17.25, 19)" leg length (customizable) and desired foot length

YARN
Hawthorne™ (fingering weight, 80% Fine Superwash Highland Wool, 20% Polyamide (Nylon); 357 yards/100g): MC Cattail Kettle 28620, 1 (2, 2) hank(s); CC Turkish Delight Kettle 26691, 1 hank

NEEDLES
US 1 (2.5mm) DPNs or two circular needles for two circulars technique or 32" or longer circular needle for Magic Loop technique, or size to obtain gauge

NOTIONS
Stitch Markers
Yarn Needle

GAUGE
32 sts and 44 rnds = 4" in Stockinette Stitch, blocked

For pattern support, contact mone.draeger@web.de

Seamless Seam Socks

Notes:
Inspired by classic seamed stockings, this minimalistic design uses a single line of knit stitches in a contrast color to mimic a seam at the back of the leg. The seam leads neatly into the integrated heel, worked also in contrast color.

These knee-high socks are worked from the cuff down. The calf is shaped for a good fit. The heel is integrated into the leg and is worked in intarsia in the round technique.

The integrated heel section has to be worked in full to achieve the correct number of stitches for the heel turn. The section adds approximately 2.5 (3, 3.25)" to the total leg length. To shorten or lengthen the leg, work fewer or more rnds in St st before the integrated heel section.

When changing yarns within a round, always pick up the yarn as indicated in the pattern to avoid holes.

1x1 Twisted Rib
Rnd 1: (K1 TBL, P1) to end.
Rep Rnd 1 for pattern.

Intarsia in the Round
The heel section is worked using an intarsia in the round method. The term 'in the round' is actually misleading, because the work is done in rows: one RS knit row across all sts is followed by a WS purl row across all sts. Because always all sts are worked, the term 'rounds' is used nevertheless. The rnds are connected by a specific step at the end of the rnd to make the piece seamless. The method in this pattern uses a YO at the beginning of every round, which at the end of the round is worked together with the last st. Using the last regular st and the YO created at the beginning of the rnd, finish each RS rnd with an SSK and finish each WS rnd with a P2tog as instructed.

LLI (Left Lifted Increase)
Knit into the left shoulder of the st two below the st on the RH needle.

DIRECTIONS

Cuff
Using your choice of stretchy cast on method, with CC, CO 72 (84, 96) sts and join for working in the rnd, being careful not to twist sts. PM for BOR.
Work 1x1 Twisted Rib until piece measures 2" from CO edge.

Leg
Join MC.
Rnd 1: With CC, K1; with MC, K to end.
Rnd 2: Pick up CC from below MC and with CC, K1; with MC, K to end.
Rep Rnd 2 until piece measures 7 (7.5, 8)" from CO edge.

Dec Rnd: Pick up CC from below MC and with CC, K1; with MC, K2tog, K to last 2 sts, SSK. 2 sts dec.
Rep Dec Rnd every eight rnds once, then every six rnds two times, then every four rnds 4 (6, 8) times. 56 (64, 72) sts.

WE as established, keeping first st in CC and all other sts in MC, until piece measures 12.5 (14.25, 15.75)" from CO edge.

Integrated Heel in Intarsia Technique
Setup Rnd (RS, partial rnd): Remove BOR M, with CC, KFB, LLI, turn. 2 sts inc.
Rnd 1 (WS): With CC, YO, P all CC sts, pick up MC from below CC and with MC, P to last MC st, P2tog, turn.
Rnd 2: With MC, YO, K all MC sts, pick up CC from below MC and with CC, K1, M1R, K to last CC st, M1L, SSK, turn. 2 sts inc.
Rep Rnds 1-2 another 12 (14, 16) times; then rep Rnd 1 once more. 84 (96, 108) sts.
Next Rnd (RS, partial rnd): With MC, Sl1, K all MC sts. Do not turn at end of rnd. Do not break MC.

Heel Turn
The heel turn will be worked over the first 43 (49, 55) sts of rnd and the last 14 (16, 18) sts of rnd just worked. Hold remaining 27 (31, 35) sts for instep either on working needles or transfer to st holder or scrap yarn if preferred.
Short Row 1 (RS): With CC, K18 (20, 22), K2tog, K1, turn. 1 st dec.
Short Row 2 (WS): With CC, Sl1 WYIF, P8, P2tog TBL, P1, turn. 1 st dec.
Short Row 3: With CC, Sl1 WYIB, K to 1 st before gap, K2tog, K1, turn. 1 st dec.
Short Row 4: With CC, Sl1 WYIF, P to 1 st before gap, P2tog TBL, P1, turn. 1 st dec.
Rep Short Rows 3-4 another 3 (4, 5) times. 47 (53, 59) heel sts; 19 (21, 23) sts between the gaps; 74 (84, 94) sts total. Break CC.
Pick up MC and using MC rep Short Rows 3-4 another 5 (6, 7) times. 37 (41, 45) heel sts; 29 (33, 37) sts between the gaps; 64 (72, 80) sts total.
Next Short Row (RS): Sl1 WYIB, K to 1 st before gap, K2tog, turn. 1 st dec.
Next Short Row (WS): Sl1 WYIF, P to 1 st before gap, P2tog TBL, turn. 1 st dec.
Rep last two Short Rows two more times; then rep RS Short Row once more. Do not turn after last row. 30 (34, 38) sole sts, 27 (31, 35) instep sts; 57 (65, 73) sts total.

Foot
Place held instep sts back on needle(s) if needed. Resume working in the rnd.
Setup Rnd: K across 27 (31, 35) instep sts, PM for BOR.
Rnd 1: SSK, K to end. 27 (31, 35) instep sts, 29 (33, 37) sole sts; 56 (64, 72) sts total.
Work St st until foot measures 1.75 (2, 2.5)" shorter than desired finished length, measured from back of heel to live sts. Break MC.

Toe
Join CC.

Rnds 1-3: K all.

Rnd 4: K1, SSK, K23 (27, 31), K2tog, K1, PM, K to end. 27 (31, 35) sts each on instep and sole; 54 (62, 70) sts total.

Rnds 5-6: K all.

Rnd 7: (K1, SSK, K to 3 sts before M, K2tog, K1) two times. 4 sts dec.

Rnd 8: K all.

Rep Rnds 7-8 another 3 (5, 7) times. 38 sts.

Rep Rnd 7 five more times. 18 sts.

Graft instep sts to sole sts.

Second Sock
Make second sock same as first.

Finishing
Weave in ends, wash, and block as desired.

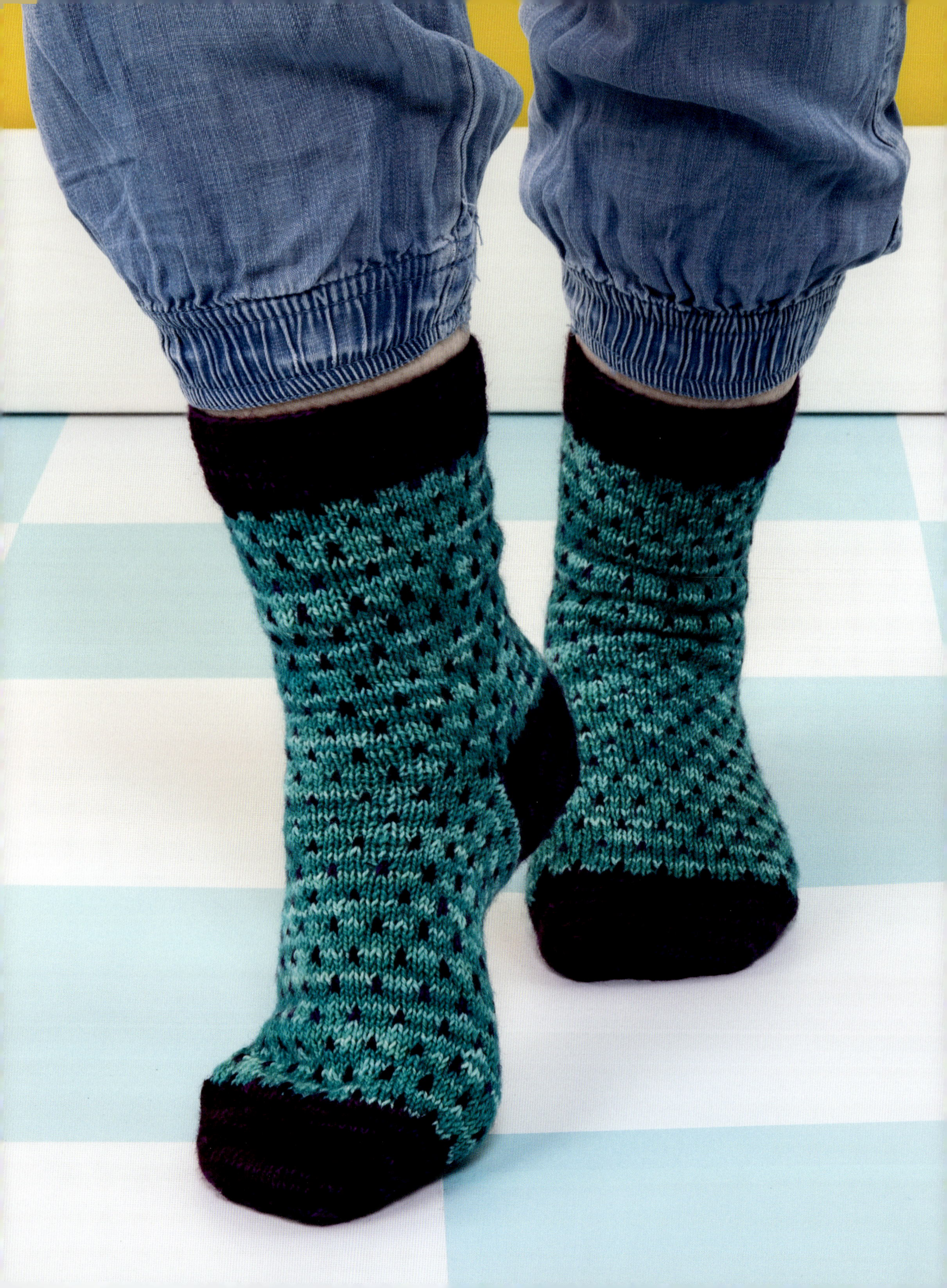

SUNBEAM SOCKS
by Amy Kate Sutherland

FINISHED MEASUREMENTS
7 (8, 9)" finished foot circumference; meant to be worn with 0–1" positive ease

YARN
Hawthorne™ (fingering weight, 80% Fine Superwash Highland Wool, 20% Polyamide (Nylon); 357 yards/100g): MC Poseidon Kettle 26693, CC Goddess Kettle 26689, 1 hank each

NEEDLES
US 1 (2.25mm) 32" circular needles, or size to obtain gauge

NOTIONS
Yarn Needle
Scrap Yarn (1 yard, high contrast)

GAUGE
32 sts and 40 rnds = 4" in Stockinette Stitch in the round, blocked

For pattern support, contact thegracefultangle@gmail.com

Sunbeam Socks

Notes:
These socks are designed as a reminder of how the smallest glimpse of sunlight instantly warms the soul. Enjoy learning a unique stitch while creating the cutest socks!

These socks feature slip-stitch colorwork. Only one color is used per round, which makes this technique perfect for those who are just starting using multiple colors in one project.

Chart is worked in the round; read each chart row from right to left as a RS row.

Sunbeam Pattern (in the round over a multiple of 4 sts)
Rnd 1: With MC, (Sl1, K3) to end.
Rnd 2: Rep Rnd 1.
Rnd 3: With MC, K all.
Rnd 4: Rep Rnd 3.
Rnd 5: With CC, (Sl2, K1, Sl1) to end.
Rnd 6: With MC, (K2, Sl1, K1) to end.
Rnd 7: Rep Rnd 6.
Rnds 8-9: Rep Rnds 3-4.
Rnd 10: With CC, (K1, Sl3) to end.
Rep Rnds 1-10 for pattern.

DIRECTIONS

Cuff
Using CC, CO 56 (64, 72) sts. Join to work in the rnd, dividing sts in half on needles for Magic Loop method. 28 (32, 36) sts on each needle.
Work 1x1 Rib for 15 rnds.

Leg
Work Rnds 1-10 of Sunbeam Pattern five times.
Work Rnds 1-8 once more. On final rnd, work across first half of sts only.

Heel Setup
Using scrap yarn, work following instructions on second half of sts only.
Row 1 (RS): K across. 28 (32, 36) sts.
Row 2 (WS): P across.
Row 3: K across.
After working Row 3, Sl all sts back to LH needle, and break scrap yarn. Pick up main yarn, and complete second half of Rnd 8 from Leg instructions.

Foot
Work Rnds 9-10 of Sunbeam Pattern, then rep Rnds 1-10 of Sunbeam Pattern as needed until foot measures 4" shorter than desired length, measured from heel setup. End on pattern Rnd 2 or Rnd 7.

Toe
Use CC.
Rnd 1: K all.
Rnd 2: (K1, SSK, K to last 3 sts on needle, K2tog, K1) two times. 4 sts dec.
Rep Rnds 1-2 nine more times. 16 (24, 32) sts.

Graft toe sts tog.

Afterthought Heel
Use CC.
Setup: With toe pointed down, from right to left PU right leg of st only of the 28 (32, 36) sts on the rows directly above and below scrap yarn, starting with sts above scrap yarn (leg), then use second needle to PU sts below (foot). Cut and remove scrap yarn between needles.
Rnd 1: K all sts, picking up an extra sts at each end of both needles to prevent gaps. 60 (68, 76) sts.
Rnd 2: *K26 (30, 34), K2tog twice; rep from * once more (on second needle). 56 (64, 72) sts.
Rnd 3: K all.
Rnd 4: (K1, SSK, K to last 3 sts on needle, K2tog, K1) two times. 4 sts dec.
Rep Rnds 3-4 nine more times. 16 (24, 32) sts.

Graft heel sts tog.

Finishing
Weave in ends, wash, and block as desired.

Sunbeam Pattern

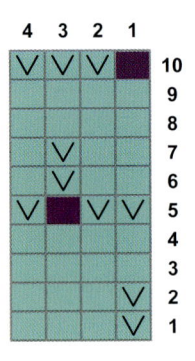

4	3	2	1	
V	V	V	■	10
				9
				8
	V			7
	V			6
V	■	V	V	5
				4
				3
			V	2
			V	1

LEGEND

■ Main Color

■ Contrasting Color

□ Knit Stitch

V Sl
Slip stitch purl-wise, with yarn in back

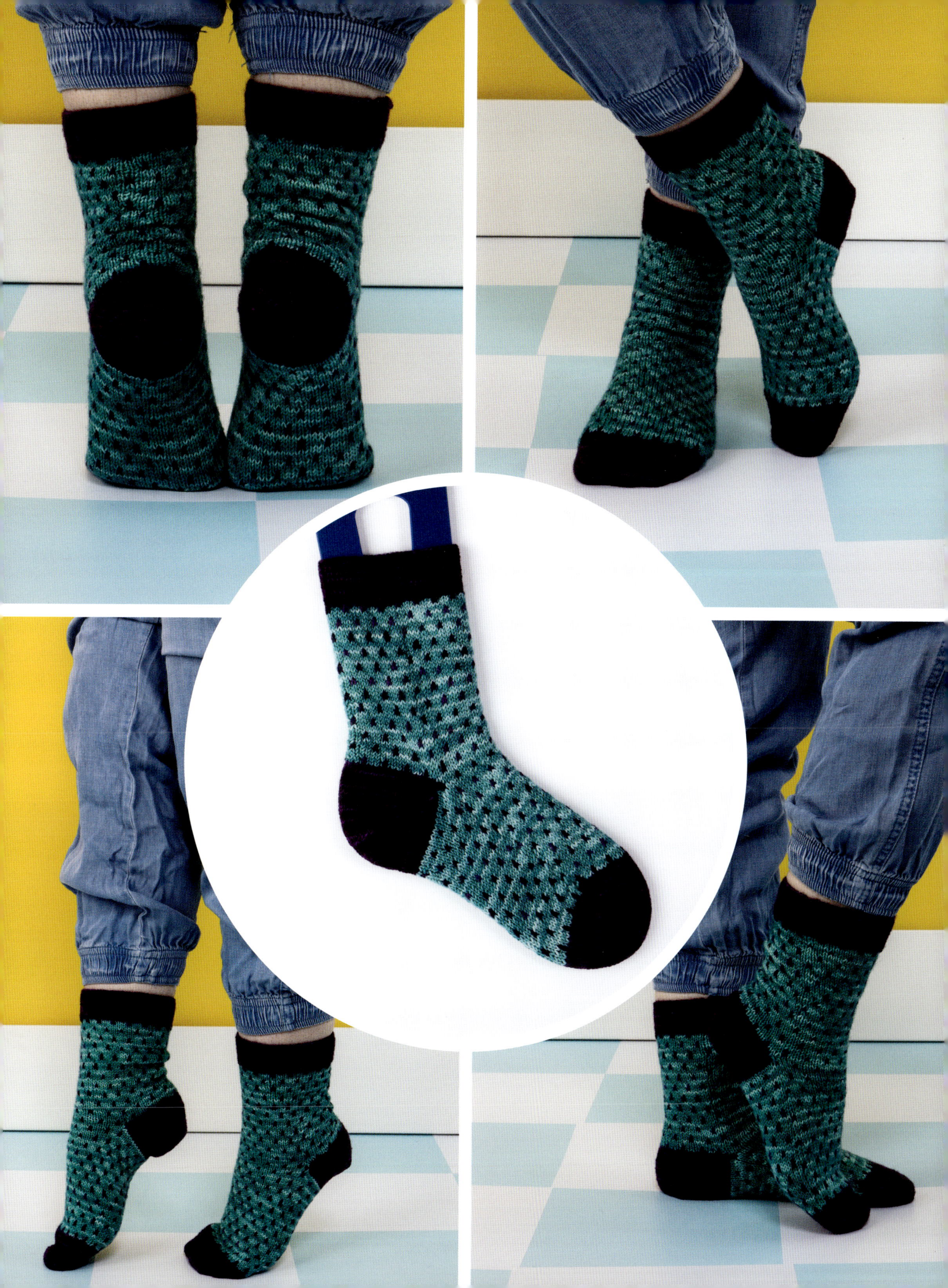

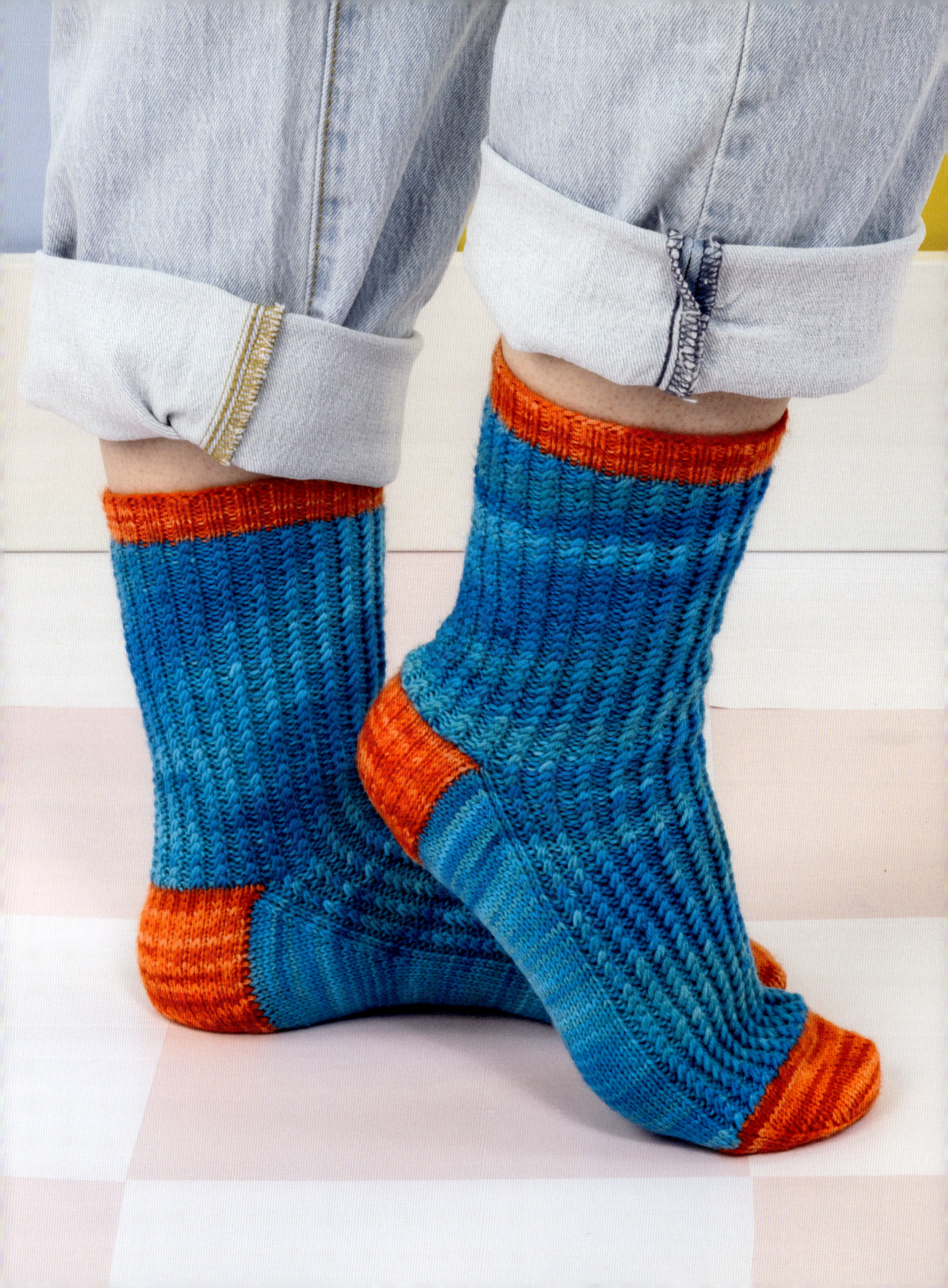

TINY TWISTS SOCKS
by Maggie McCourt

FINISHED MEASUREMENTS
9 (10.5, 12)" finished foot/leg circumference (stitch pattern is very stretchy and will stretch to fit a range of shoe sizes); length is customizable

YARN
Stroll™ Tonal (fingering weight, 75% Fine Superwash Merino Wool, 25% Nylon; 462 yards/100g): MC Blue Yonder 24906, CC Guppy 28266, 1 hank each

NEEDLES
US 1 (2.25mm) DPNs or two circular needles for two circulars technique or 32" or longer circular needles for Magic Loop technique, or size to obtain gauge

NOTIONS
Yarn Needle
Stitch Markers

GAUGE
32 sts and 48 rnds = 4" in Stockinette Stitch in the round, blocked
48 sts and 48 rnds = 4" in Tiny Twist Pattern, blocked

For pattern support, contact maggiemc1900@protonmail.com

Tiny Twists Socks

Notes:
Socks are a lovely gift, and for those who like to keep gifts a secret beforehand, the stretchiness of these socks means they'll fit a very wide variety of people. The Right Twists also provide a bit of pizazz for those who don't want to knit a plain ribbed sock.

This project is worked in the round with a small circumference, with a heel flap and gusset, wedge toe, and is grafted closed.

RT (Right Twist, without a cable needle)
With RH needle in front of work, K second st on LH needle without sliding sts off LH needle, K first st on LH needle, then slide both sts off LH needle.

Tiny Twist Pattern (in the round over a multiple of 3 sts)
Rnd 1: (P1, K2) to end.
Rnd 2: (P1, RT) to end.
Rep Rnds 1-2 for pattern.

DIRECTIONS

Cuff
With CC, CO 72 (84, 96) sts. Join to work in the rnd, being careful not to twist sts; PM for BOR.
Rnd 1: (P1, K2) to end.
Rep Rnd 1 eight more times with CC, then once with MC.

Leg
With MC, work Tiny Twist Pattern until leg is 6" or desired length, ending on pattern Rnd 2. Do not break MC yarn.

Heel Flap
Heel flap is worked in CC, flat over 36 (42, 48) sts.
Turn work and join CC.
Row 1 (WS): Sl1, P35 (41, 47).
Row 2 (RS): (Sl1, K1) to end of heel sts.
Rep Rows 1-2 another 16 (20, 24) times

Heel Turn
Short Row 1 (WS): Sl1, P18 (21, 24), P2tog, P1, turn. 35 (41, 47) sts.
Short Row 2 (RS): Sl1, K4, SSK, K1, turn. 34 (40, 46) sts dec.
Short Row 3: Sl1, P to 1 st before gap, P2tog, P1, turn. 1 st dec.
Short Row 4: Sl1, K to 1 st before gap, SSK, K1, turn. 1 st dec.
Rep Short Rows 3-4 another 7 (8, 10) times. For final Row 4, you will be unable to work last K1. 20 (24, 26) heel sts.

Gusset
Rnd 1: With CC, PU and K 18 (22, 26) sts, break CC and switch to MC, work 36 (42, 48) sts in Rnd 1 of Tiny Twist Pattern as established, PU and P 1 st, PM, PU and K 18 (22, 26) sts, K38 (46, 42), PM for BOR. 92 (110, 116) sts.
Rnd 2: Work Rnd 2 of Tiny Twist Pattern as established to M, SM, K1, SSK, K to last 3 sts, K2tog, K1. 2 sts dec.
Rnd 3: Work Rnd 1 of Tiny Twist Pattern to M, SM, K to end.
Rep Rnds 2-3 another 9 (12, 14) times. 72 (84, 96) sts.

Foot
Cont working Tiny Twist Pattern (instep) and St st (sole) as established until sock is 6 (7, 8)" or 2 (2.25, 2.5)" shorter than desired length.
Break MC.

Toe
Join CC.
Rnd 1: K1, PM for new BOR, K36 (42, 48), PM, K36 (42, 48) to end.
Rnd 2: (K1, SSK, K to 3 sts before M, K2tog, K1) two times. 4 sts dec.
Rnd 3: K to M, SM, K to end.
Rep Rnds 2-3 another 9 (10, 12) times, then work Rnd 2 another 5 (6, 6) times. 12 (16, 20) sts.

Graft toe sts closed.

Second Sock
Make second sock same as first.

Finishing
Weave in ends, wash, and block as desired.

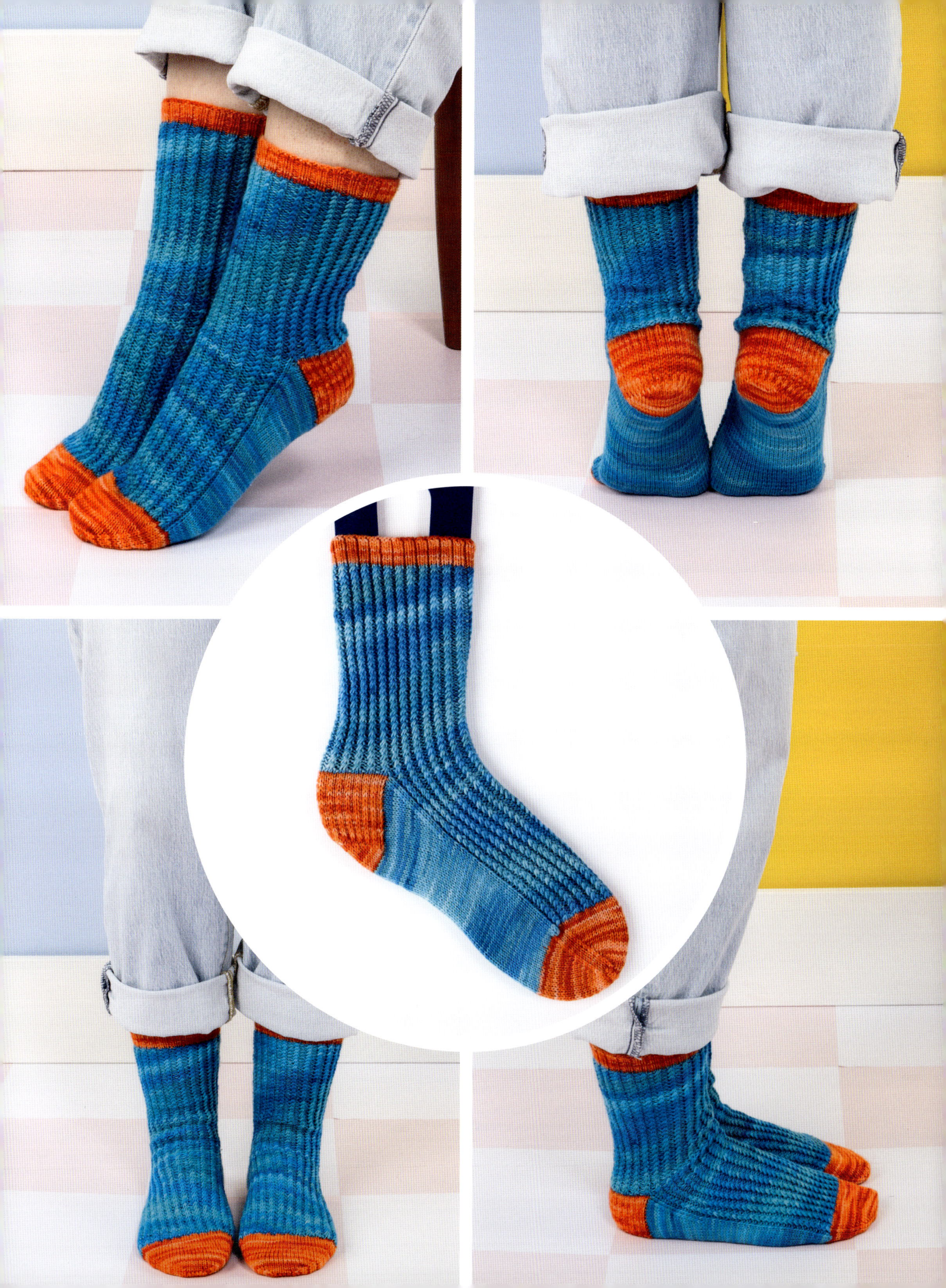

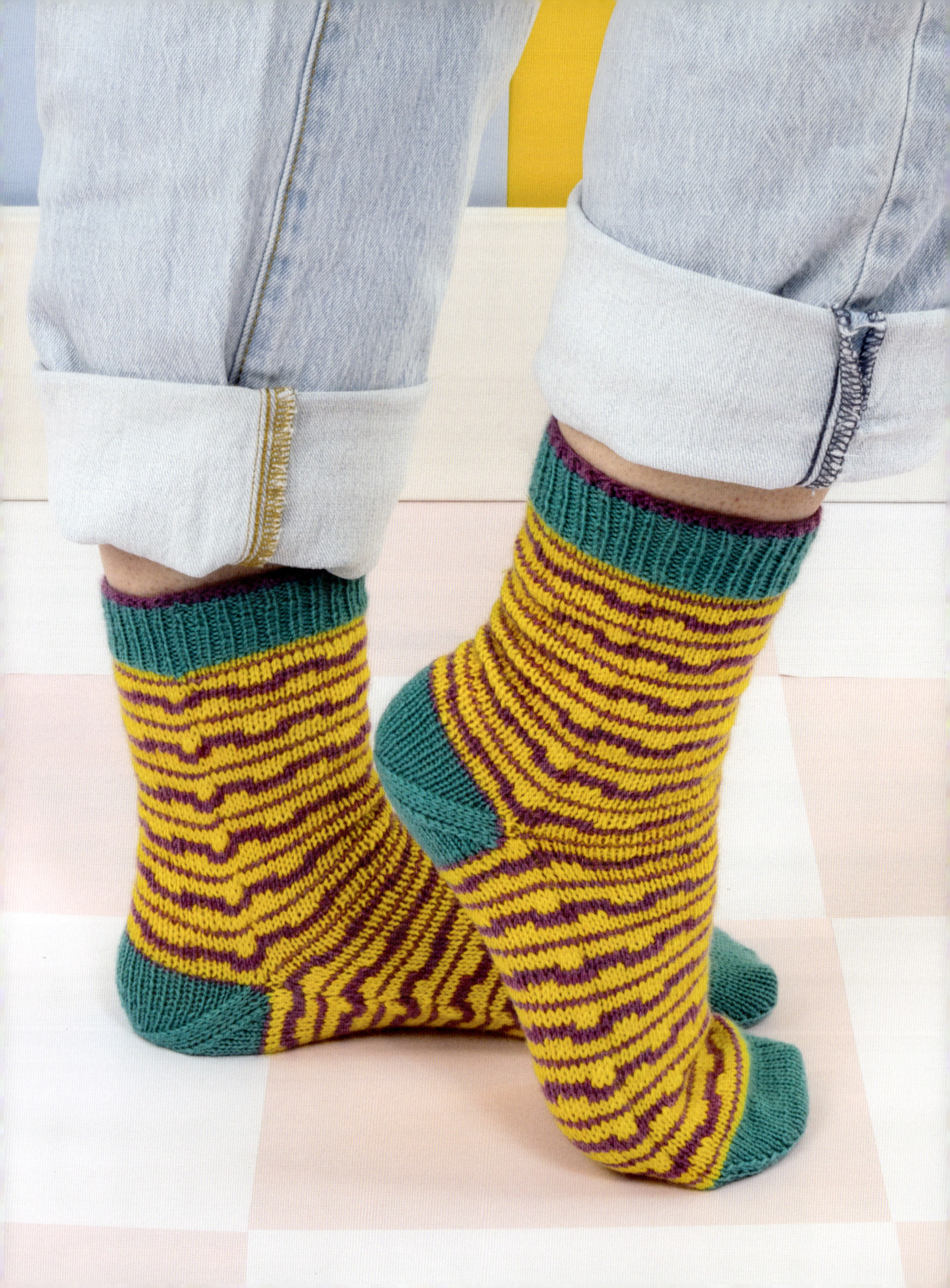

WAVY STRIPES SOCKS
by Jennifer Beaulieu

FINISHED MEASUREMENTS
7 (8, 9)" circumference × adjustable foot length; meant to be worn with approx 10% negative ease

YARN
Stroll™ (fingering weight, 75% Fine Superwash Merino Wool, 25% Nylon; 231 yards/50g): C1 Paisley Heather 28187, C2 Dandelion 25024, C3 Patina 28181, 1 skein each
(tutorial photos use C1 Pucker 26401 and C2 Dove Heather 25023)

NEEDLES
US 1 (2.25mm) DPNs or two circular needles for two circulars technique or 32" or longer circular needles for Magic Loop technique, or size to obtain gauge

NOTIONS
Yarn Needle
Locking Stitch Markers
Ruler or Tape Measure

GAUGE
34 sts and 44 rnds = 4" in Wavy Stripes Pattern in the round, blocked

For pattern support, contact ellyndriaknits@gmail.com

Wavy Stripes Socks

Notes:
Stripes are so compelling to knit, it is hard to stop! Thin stripes alternate with slightly thicker wavy stripes for visual interest, while the cuff, heels, and toes add a pop of color. A small stripe at the beginning of the cuff completes the look.

These socks are knit from the cuff down, with minimal stranded colorwork throughout the leg and foot, perfect for the beginning colorwork knitter. A cut-in afterthought heel is worked on the back of the first sock, while the second sock's heel is worked on the front: when flipped, the BOR falls to the inside of the leg on both socks.

Parts of the pattern are written for two needles, with stitches divided perfectly in half between a front needle and a back needle. If using DPNs, divide four needles so that the first two are considered the "front needle" and the last two are the "back needle".

Chart is worked in the round; read each chart row from right to left as a RS row.

Wavy Stripes Pattern (in the round over a multiple of 8 sts)
Rnd 1: With C1, K all.
Rnds 2-3: With C2, K all.
Rnd 4: (With C1, K5; with C2, K3) to end.
Rnd 5: With C1, K all.
Rnd 6: (With C1, K1; with C2, K3; with C1, K4) to end.
Rnds 7-8: With C2, K all.
Rep Rnds 1-8 for pattern.

DIRECTIONS

Cuff
With C1, CO 56 (64, 72) sts using a German Twisted Cast On or other long tail cast on method. Join to work in the rnd, being careful not to twist sts; PM for BOR.
Rnd 1: (K1, P1) to end. Break C1.
Rnd 2: With C3, K all.
Rnds 3-16: (K1, P1) to end.
Break C3.

Leg
With C2, knit two rnds.
Work Rnds 1-8 of Wavy Stripes Pattern six times or until desired leg length, using chart or written instructions.
Rep pattern Rnd 1 once more.

Placing Markers for Heel
Three locking Ms are now placed through sts of the last rep of Rnd 1 completed. Alternatively, the foot and toe may be completed before measuring back to PMs. These Ms indicate the row that will be cut into and removed.

Looking at the 28 (32, 36) sts on back of sock (for first sock), or on front of sock (for second sock), and assuming they are all on one needle, PMs as follows.

1. Place first M through first st on needle.
2. Place second M through last st on needle.
3. Place third M through one of the 2 center sts.

Foot
Beginning with Rnd 2 of Wavy Stripes Pattern, cont knitting in pattern until sock measures 4″ shorter than desired foot length, ending foot after knitting a Rnd 3 of pattern.
Break C1 and C2.

Note: Additional length may be added by knitting plain rnds in C3 if ending after Rnd 3 does not meet required foot length.

Toe
Setup: With C3, knit two rnds.
Rnd 1: (K1, SSK, K to last 3 sts on needle, K2tog, K1) two times. 4 sts dec.
Rnd 2: K all.
Rep Rnds 1-2 another 6 (7, 8) times. 28 (32, 36) sts.
Rep Rnd 1 another 3 (4, 4,) times. 16 (16, 20) sts.

Graft toe sts closed.

Heel
If Ms for heel have not yet been placed, using ruler or tape measure, measure from end of toe to 2″ shorter than desired foot length, and place Ms in nearest Rnd 1 that does not exceed this length. Refer to Place Markers for Heel; because those sts are no longer on a needle, count to make sure Ms are placed in the first and 28th (32nd, 36th) sts.

Picking Up Stitches for Heel
Looking at side of sock where Ms were placed, and starting with st marked by first M and ending with st marked by last M: On row immediately above Ms, take needle and PU right leg of each st in that row. 28 (32, 36) sts. If using a circular needle, pull needle through so sts rest on cable.
(See photo 1.)

On row immediately below Ms, take second needle and PU right leg of each st in row. 28 (32, 36) sts. Again, if using a circular needle, pull needle through so sts rest on cable.
(See photo 2.)
56 (64, 72) sts.
Make sure both needles are pointing in same direction. Remove outer two Ms.

Making the Cut
After all heel sts are on needles, pull up on middle M for heel. Taking a small, pointy pair of scissors, snip only one leg of marked st.
(See photo 3.)
Using a yarn needle, slowly unpick row of sts, one leg at a time. Do not unpick last 2 sts on either end of that row, as these 2 sts will help prevent holes.
(See photos 4 and 5.)

After row is unpicked, tuck both yarn ends inside hole created. When weaving in ends later, those ends can help close any holes that may appear.

Knitting the Heel
Setup Rnd 1: With C1, K all. Break C1.
Setup Rnd 2: With C3, K all.

If more depth is needed for heel, knit one to three more rnds before decreasing. If plain knit rnds inc length of foot too much, the dec rnds can be stopped a few rnds early.
Rnd 1: (K1, SSK, K to last 3 sts on needle, K2tog, K1) two times. 4 sts dec.
Rnd 2: K all.
Rep Rnds 1–2 another 6 (7, 8) times. 28 (32, 36) sts.
Rep Rnd 1 another 3 (4, 4) times. 16 (16, 20) sts.

Graft heel sts closed.

Second Sock
Make second sock, paying attention to heel marker placement.

Finishing
Weave in ends, wash, and block as desired.

Wavy Stripes Pattern

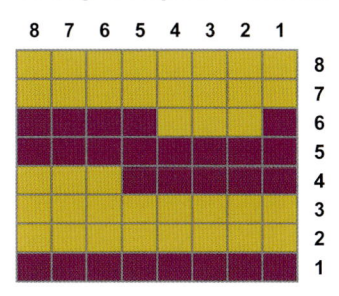

8	7	6	5	4	3	2	1	
								8
								7
C1	C1	C1		C1	C1	C1	C1	6
C1	C1	C1		C1	C1	C1	C1	5
C1	C1		C1	C1	C1	C1	C1	4
C1	C1		C1	C1	C1	C1	C1	3
								2
								1

LEGEND

■ Color 1

■ Color 2

□ Knit Stitch

Photo 1: First row picked up

Photo 2: All sts picked up

Photo 3: Middle st ready to be cut

Photo 4: Starting to unpick

Photo 5: First side unpicked

Wavy Stripes Socks

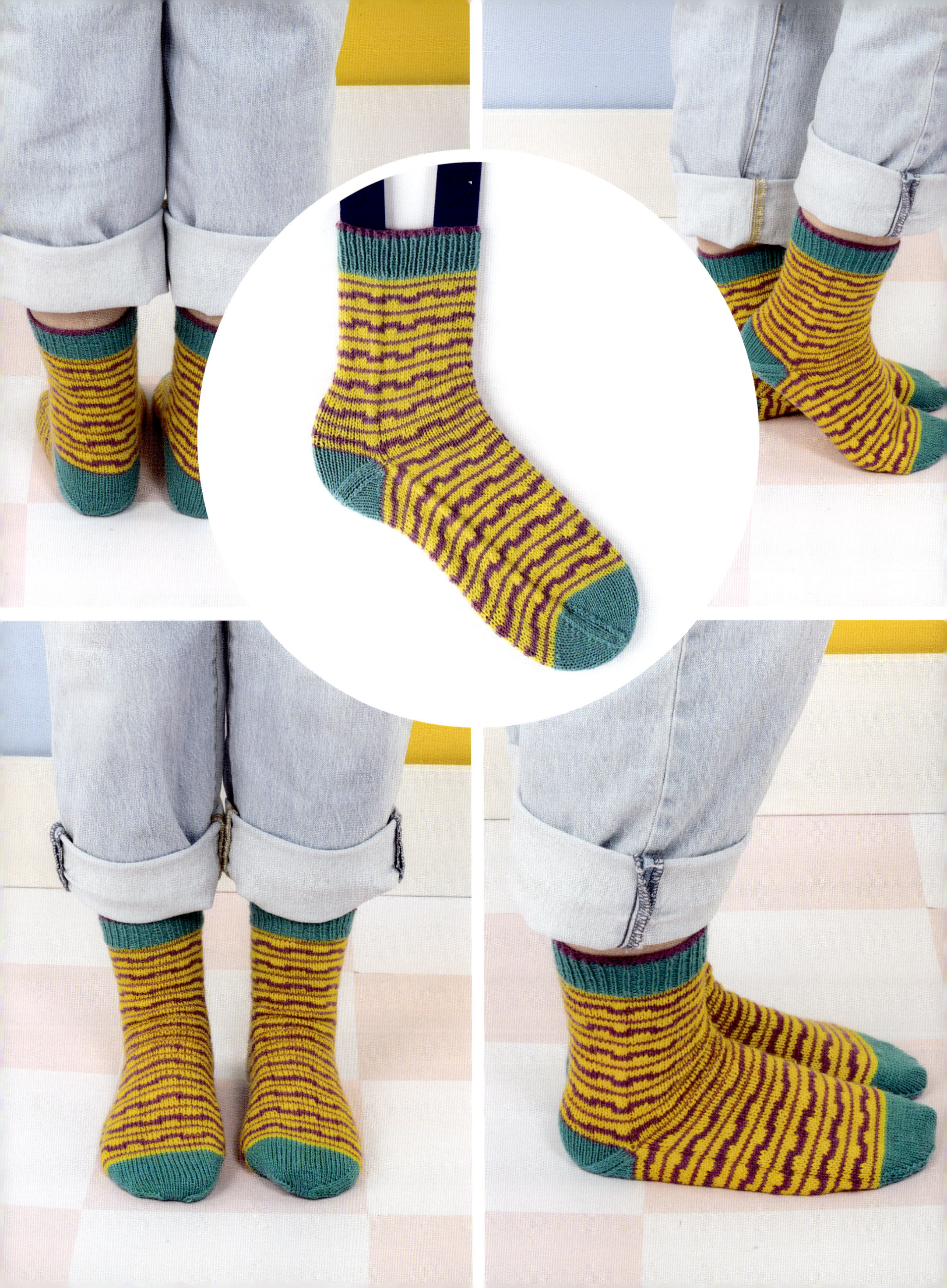

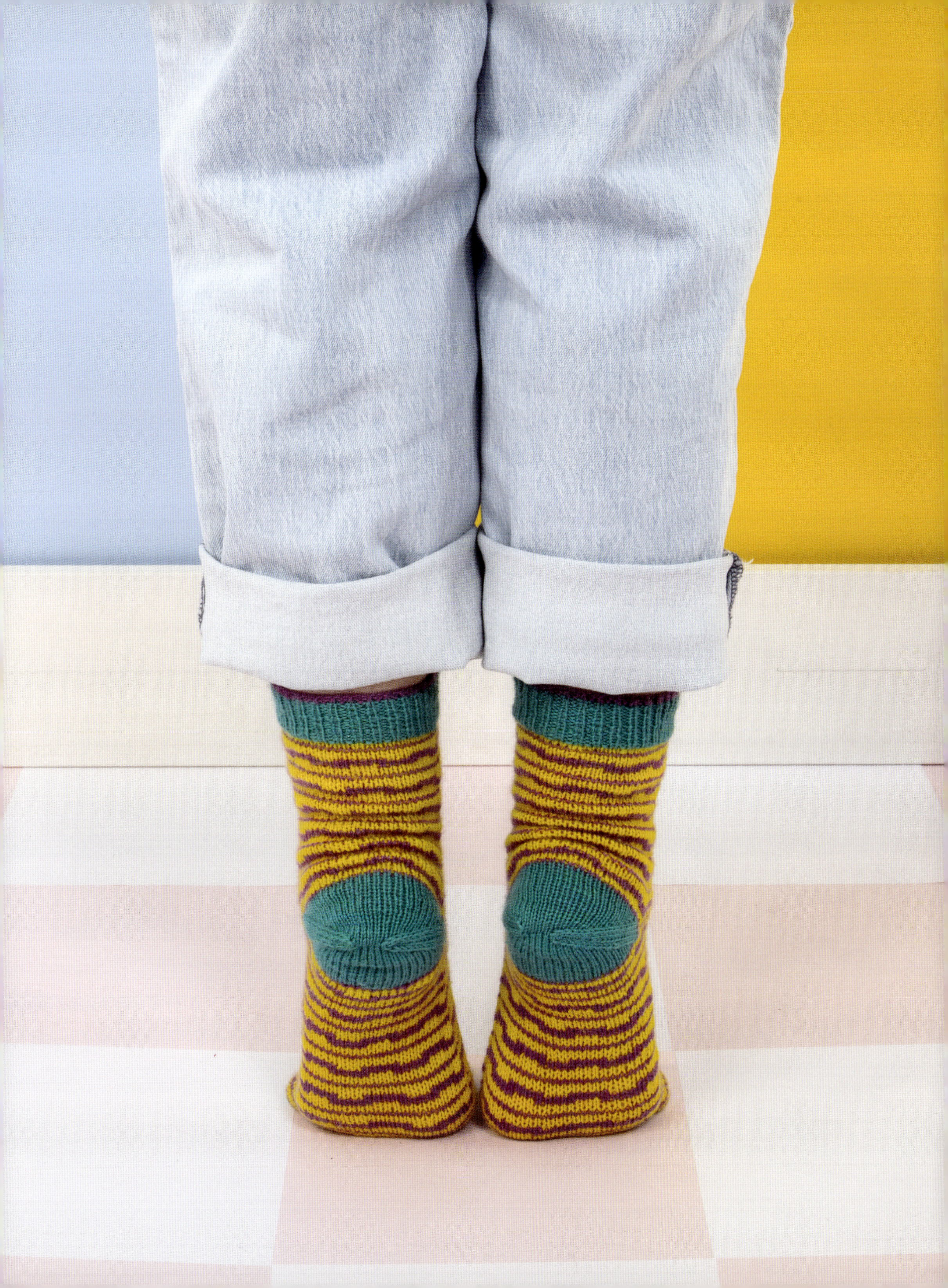

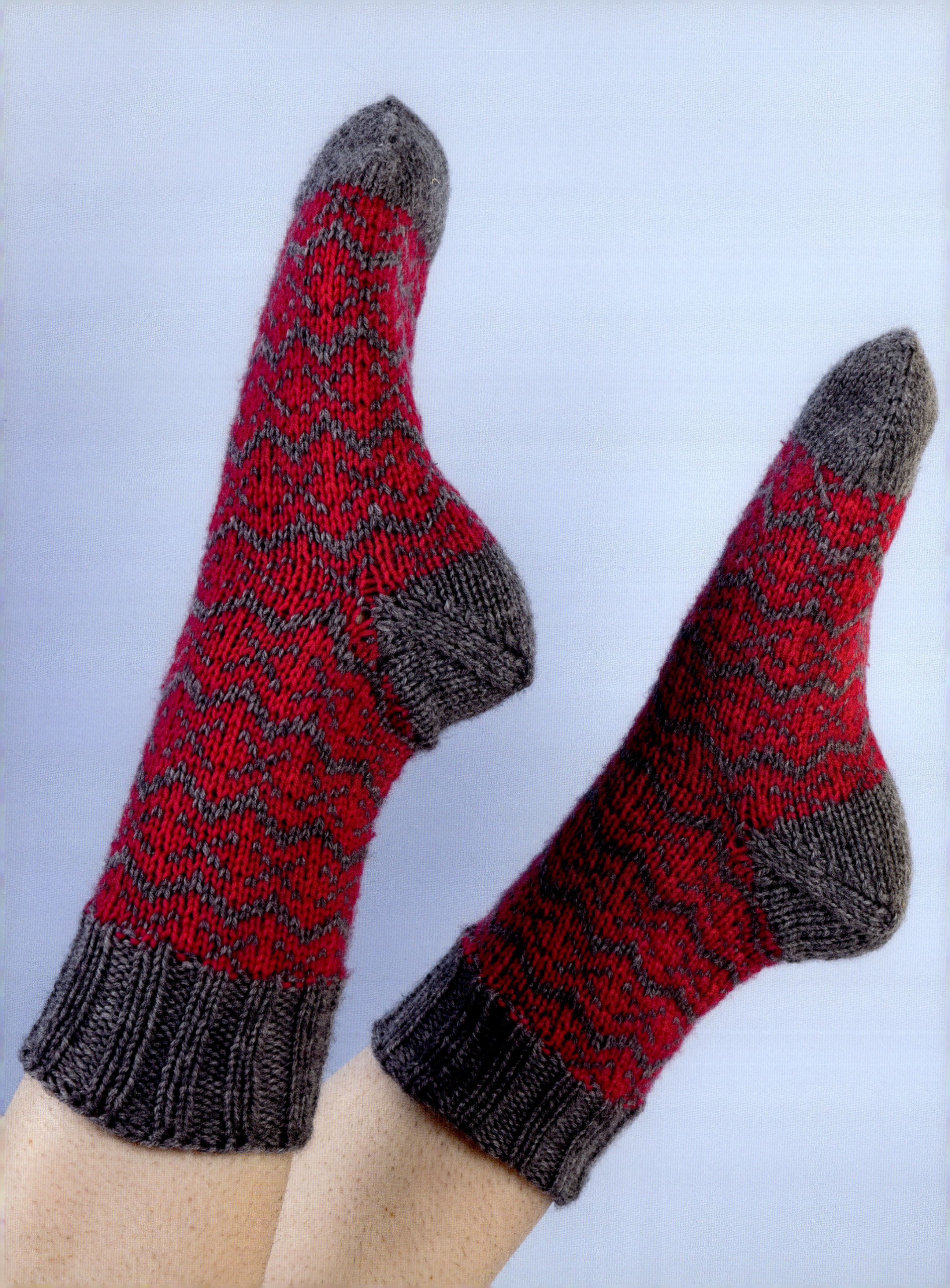

WAYFINDER'S SOCKS
by Francoise Danoy

FINISHED MEASUREMENTS
7.5 (9)" finished foot circumference; meant to be worn with 1" negative ease; length can be worked to desired measurements

YARN
Swish™ (DK weight, 100% Fine Superwash Merino Wool; 123 yards/50g): MC Marble Heather 24636, CC Crush 28640, 1 skein each

NEEDLES
US 5 (3.75mm) DPNs or two circular needles for two circulars technique or 32" or longer circular needles for Magic Loop technique, or size to obtain gauge

US 6 (4mm) DPNs or two circular needles for two circulars technique or 32" or longer circular needles for Magic Loop technique, or one size larger than size used to obtain gauge

NOTIONS
Yarn Needle
Removeable Stitch Markers
Scrap Yarn

GAUGE
26 sts and 32 rnds = 4" in Stockinette Stitch in the round, blocked, on smaller needles

For pattern support, contact fdanoy@arohaknits.com

Wayfinder's Socks

Notes:

The colorwork motif on these socks is inspired by traditional Māori motifs. The Xs represent the stars in the night sky, while the chevrons represent the ocean waves. Wayfinders would use the stars to navigate the vast ocean seas.

This pattern is a great intro to basic sock knitting, as it features commonly used techniques such as Judy's Magic Cast On, the Afterthought Heel, and grafting.

Chart is worked in the round; read each chart row from right to left as a RS row.

Wayfinder Pattern (in the round over a multiple of 6 sts)
Rnd 1: With CC, K1; with MC, K1; with CC, K3; with MC, K1.
Rnd 2: With CC, K2; (with MC, K1; with CC, K1) two times.
Rnd 3: With CC, K3; with MC, K1; with CC, K2.
Rnd 4: Rep Rnd 2.
Rnd 5: Rep Rnd 1.
Rnd 6: Rep Rnd 3.
Rnd 7: With CC, K2; with MC, K3; with CC, K1.
Rnd 8: (With CC, K1; with MC, K2) two times.
Rnd 9: With MC, K2; with CC, K3; with MC, K1.
Rnd 10: With MC, K1; with CC, K5.
Rnd 11: Rep Rnd 2.
Rnd 12: Rep Rnd 1.
Rnd 13: Rep Rnd 10.
Rnd 14: Rep Rnd 1.
Rnd 15: Rep Rnd 2.
Rnd 16: Rep Rnd 10.
Rnd 17: Rep Rnd 9.
Rnd 18: Rep Rnd 8.
Rnd 19: Rep Rnd 7.
Rnd 20: Rep Rnd 3.
Rep Rnds 1-20 for pattern.

DIRECTIONS

Toe
Using smaller needles, MC, and Judy's Magic Cast On, CO 6 sts per needle, 12 sts total.
Knit one rnd.

Rnd 1: *KFB, K to last st of needle, KFB; rep from * for back needle. 8 sts per needle; 16 sts total. Use a detachable stitch marker and attach to front of sock to indicate front side.
Rnds 2-3: *KFB, K to last st of needle, KFB; rep from * for back needle. 12 sts per needle; 24 sts total.
Rnd 4: K all.
Rnd 5: *KFB, K to last st of needle, KFB; rep from * for back needle. 14 sts per needle; 28 sts total.
Rep Rnds 4-5 another 5 (8) times. 24 (30) sts per needle; 48 (60) sts total.

Work St st until sock measures approx 2.25" from tip of toe.

Foot
Switch to larger needles and join CC yarn; work Wayfinder Chart Rows 1-20 until sock measures 2" shorter than total foot length desired.

Afterthought Heel Setup
Working in pattern as established, work across front needle so that sts on back needle are ready to be worked. Place a removable M into first and last sts of back needle. Using contrasting scrap yarn, K across needle. Loosely tie tails of scrap yarn tog and tuck into sock to keep them out of the way. Sl all scrap yarn sts just worked back onto LH needle. With working yarns, K1, PM onto this st, work in pattern as established across needle and PM into last st.

Leg
Cont in pattern as established until work measures 2" for a short ankle sock or 5" for a standard length, from scrap yarn row. Break CC yarn, leaving a 6" tail.

Cuff
With smaller needles and MC, work 2x2 Rib for 2.5".
BO using Stretchy Bind Off.

Afterthought Heel
Begin with sock toe pointing downwards. You'll be working from right to left, starting with marked st.
With smaller needle, PU right leg of all sts immediately below corresponding sts worked in scrap yarn. Remove Ms when reached. Rotate work so sock toe is pointing upwards. PU right leg of all sts below scrap yarn, starting with marked st, as before. There are now 24 (30) sts on each needle; 48 (60) sts total.
Remove scrap yarn using yarn needle. This will form a hole for heel.
With sock toe pointing downwards and using MC, adjust needles to begin working in the rnd, with front and back needles.
Rnd 1: *K to end of front needle; PU 2 sts to close gap between needles; rep from * for back needle. 26 (32) sts per needle; 52 (64) sts total.
Rnd 2: K all.
Rnd 3: *K to last 4 sts of needle, K2tog twice; rep from * for second needle. 24 (30) sts per needle; 48 (60) sts total.
Rnd 4: K all.
Rnd 5: *K1, K2tog, K to last 3 sts of needle, K2tog, K1; rep from * for back needle. 4 sts dec.
Rnd 6: K all.
Rep Rnds 5-6 six more times. 10 (16) sts per needle.

Graft heel sts closed.

Second Sock
Make second sock same as first.

Finishing
Weave in ends, wash, and block as desired.

Wayfinder Pattern

LEGEND

- Main Color
- Contrasting Color
- Knit Stitch

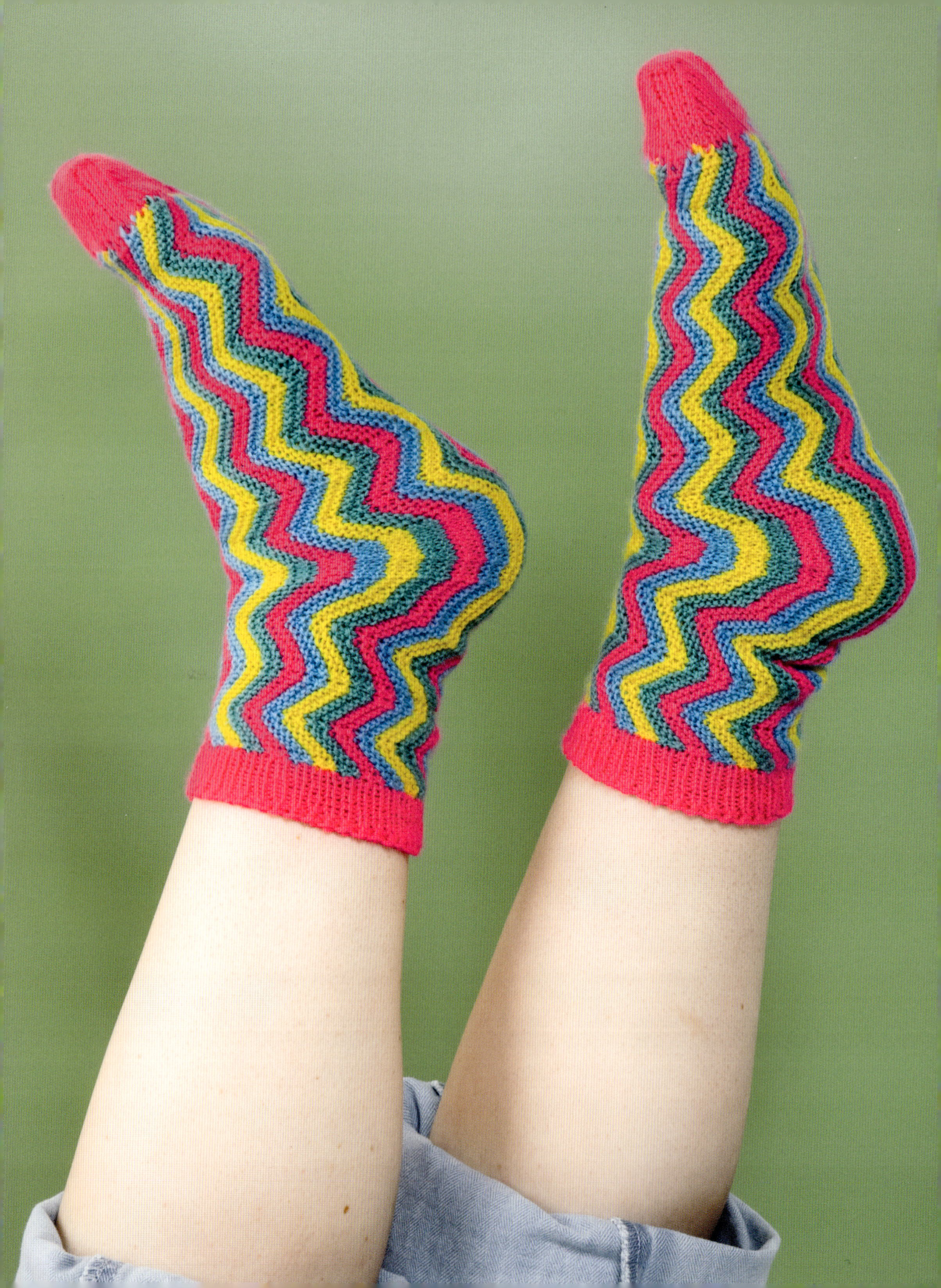

ZIGZAG SOCKS
by Irina Poludnenko

FINISHED MEASUREMENTS
7.5" leg circumference × 5.5 (7, 8.5)" foot length

YARN
Stroll™ (fingering weight, 75% Fine Superwash Merino Wool, 25% Nylon; 231 yards/50g): C1 Pucker 26401, C2 Patina 28181, C3 Dandelion 25024, C4 Electric Blue 26406, 1 skein each

NEEDLES
US 1 (2.25mm) DPNs and straight needles (or circular to work flat), or size to obtain gauge

NOTIONS
Yarn Needle
Stitch Markers
Scrap Yarn

GAUGE
44 sts and 52 rows = 4" in ZigZag Garter Stitch, blocked
28 sts and 52 rows = 4" in Garter Stitch, blocked

For pattern support, contact irina.poludnenko@gmail.com

ZigZag Socks

Notes:
This ZigZag pattern makes for a joyful knitting experience, especially for knitters who like to use different colors in unexpected ways. Knitting socks side to side is easy and gives new possibilities for the heel shaping.

These socks are worked flat side to side (foot, heel, leg) in stripes, with four rows for each color. The first and last rows are grafted together. Toe and cuff are picked up and knit on both sides of the sock.

To save time later, weave in ends as you knit.

ZigZag Garter Stitch (flat over a multiple of 16 sts)
Row 1 (RS): K2tog, K5, KFB twice, K5, K2tog.
Row 2 (WS): K across.
Rep Rows 1–2 for pattern.

DIRECTIONS
With scrap yarn and straight needles, CO 92 (108, 124) sts using a provisional cast on method of choice.

Back of Leg—First Side
Setup Row (WS): With C1, K33 (leg); PM, K12, PM, K2, PM, K12, PM (heel); K to end (foot).
Row 1 (RS): K1 (selvage st), work 2 (3, 4) reps of ZigZag Garter Stitch; SM, K12, SM, K2, SM, K12, SM; work 2 reps of ZigZag Garter Stitch; K1 (selvage st).
Row 2 (WS): K across.
With C2, rep Rows 1–2 two times.
With C3, rep Rows 1–2 two times. 11 rows worked.

Heel Shaping—First Side
Row 1 (RS): With C4, K1, work in pattern as established to M, SM, K to 2 sts before second M, K2tog, SM, K2, SM, K2tog, K to M, SM, work as established to end. 2 sts dec.
Row 2 (WS): K across.
Maintaining 4-row stripes as established (switching back to C1 after C4 is complete), rep Rows 1–2 ten more times. 70 (86, 102) sts.
Next Row (RS): K1, work as established to M, SM, remove second and third Ms and K2tog twice, SM, work as established to end. 68 (84, 100) sts.

Front of Leg
Row 1 (RS): K1, work as established to M, SM, K2, SM, work as established to end.
Row 2 (WS): K across.
Rep Rows 1–2 twelve times.

Heel Shaping—Second Side
Row 1 (RS): K1, work as established to M, SM, M1, PM, K2, PM, M1, SM, work as established to end. 70 (86, 102) sts.
Row 2 (WS): K across.
Row 3: K1, work as established to M, SM, K to M, M1, SM, K2, SM, M1, K to M, SM, work as established to end. 2 sts inc. 72, 88, 104 sts
Rep Rows 2–3 ten more times, then rep Row 2 once more. 92 (108, 124) sts.

Back of Leg—Second Side
Row 1 (RS): Work as established to M; SM, K12, SM, K2, SM, K12, SM; work as established to end.
Row 2 (WS): K across.
Rep Rows 1–2 five more times. Remove Ms on last row worked.

With C1, graft first row in C1 tog with last row. Remove scrap yarn. Place 2 Ms: one at beginning of grafted row and another at end of grafted row.

Toe
With C1 and DPNs, starting from M at beginning of grafted row, PU and K 76 sts. Join to work in the rnd and PM for BOR. Place 2 more Ms in contrasting colors: first M after first 19 sts, and second M before last 19 sts.
Rnd 1: (Work 1x1 Rib to 3 sts before M, K2tog, K1, SM, K1, SSK) two times, work 1x1 Rib to end. 4 sts dec.
Rnd 2: (Work 1x1 Rib to 2 sts before M, K2, SM, K2) two times, work 1x1 Rib to end.
Rep Rnds 1–2 four more times. 56 sts.
Rep Rnd 1 six times. 32 sts.

Place first and last 8 sts on one needle and graft tog the two sets of 16 sts.

Cuff
With C1 and DPNs, starting from M at end of grafted row, PU and K 76 sts. Join to work in the rnd and PM for BOR. Work 1x1 Rib for 1″.
BO all sts.

Second Sock
Make second sock same as first.

Finishing
Weave in remaining ends, wash, and block as desired.

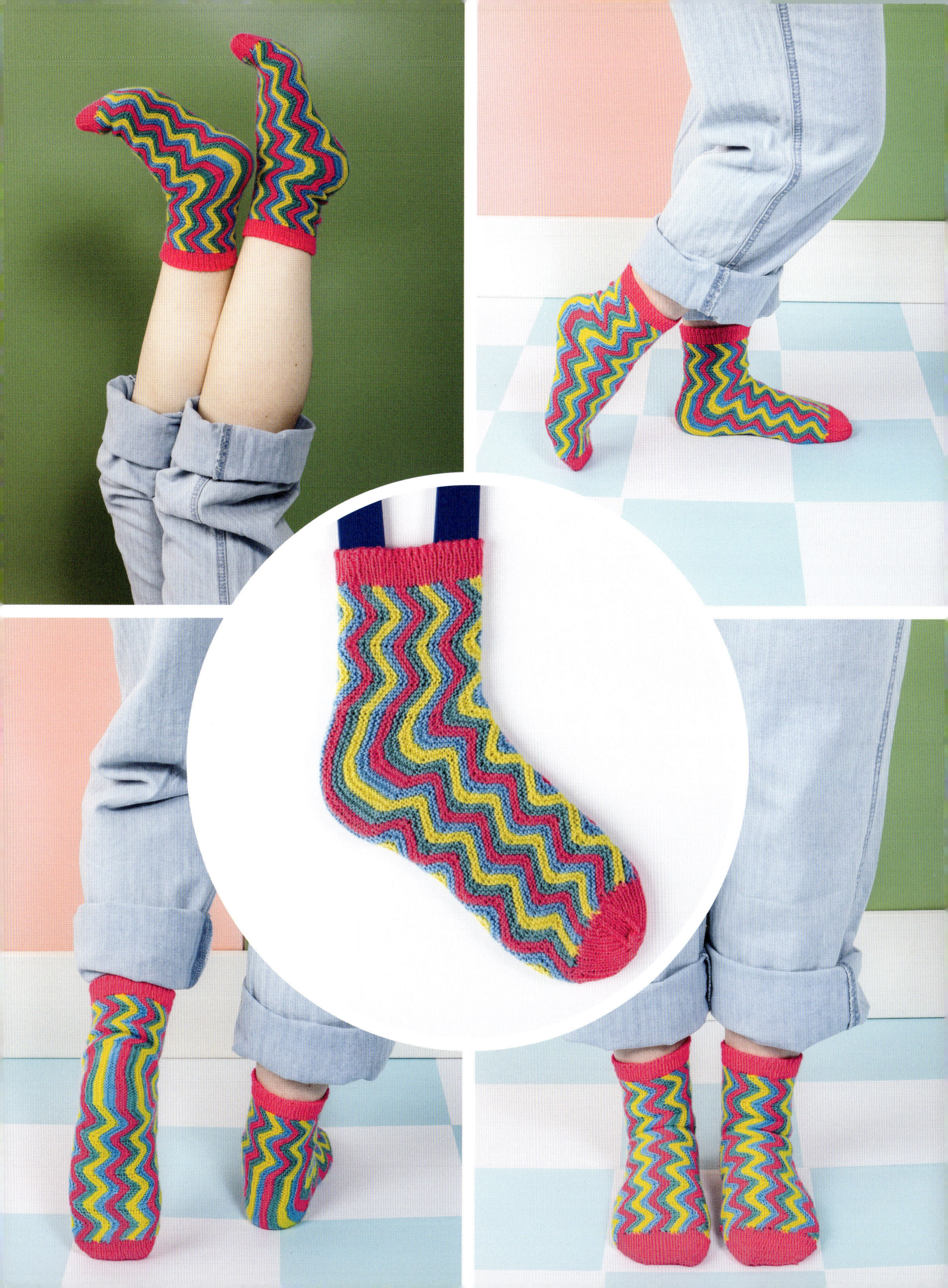

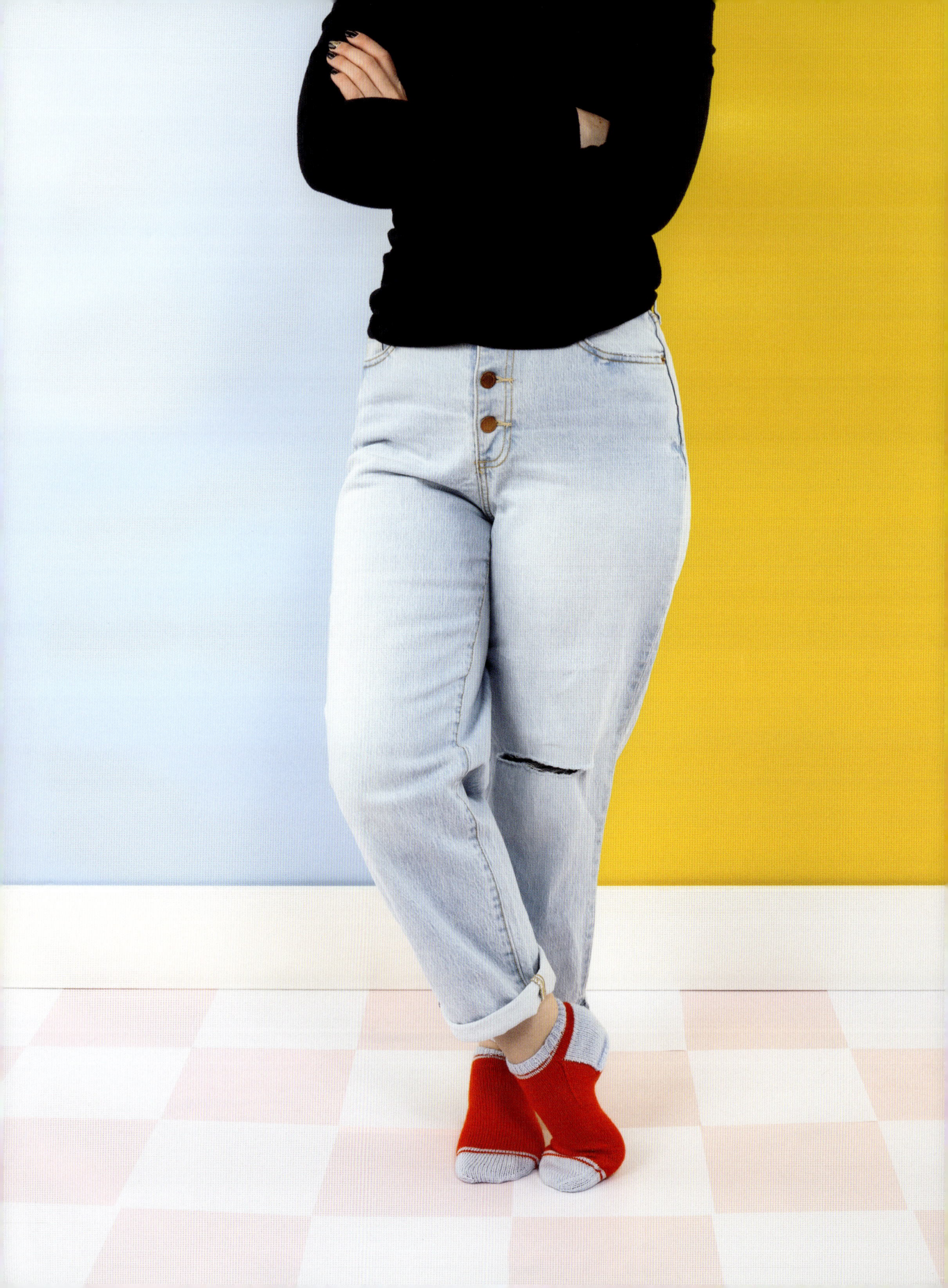

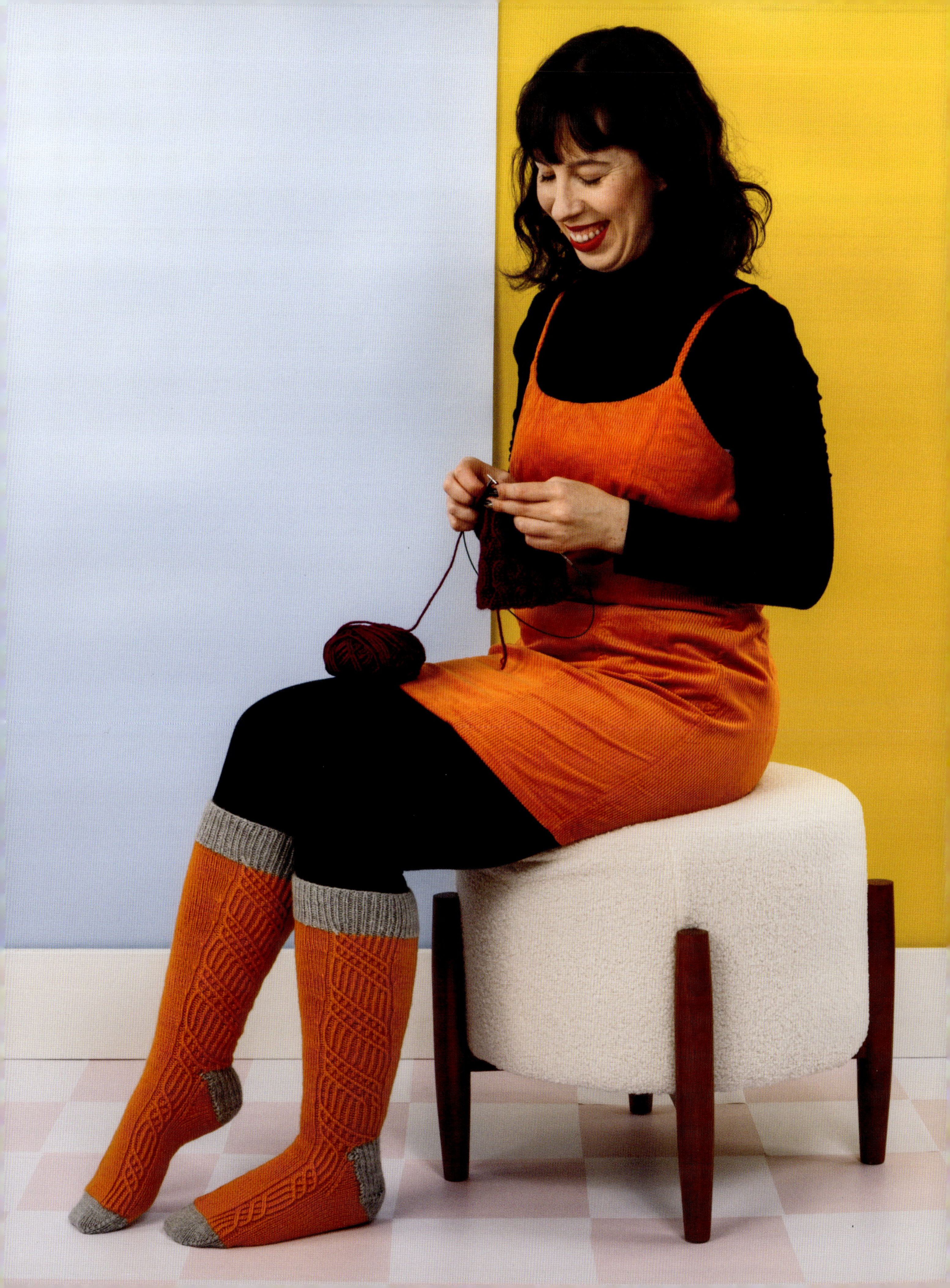

Glossary
Common Stitches & Techniques for Socks

Visit our **Learning Center** to find tons of video and photo tutorials on sock techniques! knitpicks.com/learning-center/learn-to-knit-socks.

Slipped Stitches (Sl)
Always slip stitches purl-wise with yarn held to the wrong side of work, unless noted otherwise in the pattern.

Make 1 Left-Leaning Stitch (M1L)
Inserting LH needle from front to back, PU the horizontal strand between the st just worked and the next st, and K TBL.

Make 1 Right-Leaning Stitch (M1R)
Inserting LH needle from back to front, PU the horizontal strand between the st just worked and the next st, and K TFL.

Slip, Slip, Knit (SSK)
(Sl1 K-wise) twice; insert LH needle into front of these 2 sts and knit them together.

Centered Double Decrease (CDD)
Slip first and second sts together as if to work K2tog; K1; pass 2 slipped sts over the knit st.

Stockinette Stitch (in the round over any number of sts)
Rnd 1: Knit all sts.
Rep Rnd 1 for pattern.
Rev St st is the opposite—purl all sts.

1x1 Rib (in the round over an even number of sts)
Rnd 1: (K1, P1) to end of rnd.
Rep Rnd 1 for pattern.

2x2 Rib (in the round over a multiple of 4 sts)
Rnd 1: (K2, P2) to end of rnd.
Rep Rnd 1 for pattern.

Sock Measurement Guide

US Women's Shoe Size	4-6.5	7-9.5	10-12.5
Foot length	8-9"	9.25-10"	10.25-11"
Foot Circumference	7"	8"	9"
Sock Height	6.5"	7"	7.5"

US Men's Shoe Size	6-8.5	9-11.5	12-14
Foot length	9.25-10"	10.25-11"	11.25-12"
Foot Circumference	8"	9"	10"
Sock Height	7.5"	8"	8.5"

US Children's Shoe Size	10-13	1-3	4-6
	(Child)	(Youth)	(Youth)
Foot length	6.5-7.5"	7.75-8.5"	8.75-9.5"
Foot Circumference	6"	6.5"	7"
Sock Height	4.5"	5.5"	6.5"

Knitting in the Round (Magic Loop, Two Circulars, DPNs)
The **Magic Loop technique** uses one long circular needle to knit in the round around a small circumference. The **Two Circulars technique** uses two long circular needles to knit around a small circumference. Photo and video tutorials for these, plus using **DPNs** and 16" circular needles, can be found at knitpicks.com/learning-center/knitting-in-the-round.

Tubular Cast Ons
Stretchy cast on methods with a neat looking edge for 1x1 Rib; great for starting top-down socks. A tutorial for the **Long Tail Tubular Cast On** (which does not use scrap yarn) can be found at blog.knitpicks.com/long-tail-tubular-cast-on. A tutorial for the **standard Tubular Cast On** (which uses scrap yarn that gets removed at the end) can be found at tutorials.knitpicks.com/tubular-cast-on.

Abbreviations

approx	approximately	KFB (inc 1)	knit into front and back of stitch	PSSO (dec 1)	pass slipped stitch over	SSP (dec 1)	slip, slip, purl these 2 stitches together through back loop
BO	bind off			PU	pick up		
BOR	beginning of round	K-wise	knit-wise	P-wise	purl-wise	SSSK (dec 2)	slip, slip, slip, knit these 3 stitches together (like SSK)
CN	cable needle	LH	left hand	rep	repeat		
C (1, 2…)	color (1, 2…)	M	marker	Rev St st	reverse stockinette stitch (see above)	St st	stockinette stitch (see above)
CC	contrast color	M1 (inc 1)	make 1 stitch (work same as M1L)				
CDD (dec 2)	centered double decrease (see above)	M1L (inc 1)	make 1 left-leaning stitch (see above)	RH	right hand	st(s)	stitch(es)
				rnd(s)	round(s)	TBL	through back loop
CO	cast on	M1R (inc 1)	make 1 right-leaning stitch (see above)	RS	right side	TFL	through front loop
cont	continue			Sk	skip	tog	together
dec(s)	decrease(es)	MC	main color	SK2P (dec 2)	slip K-wise, knit 2 together, pass slipped stitch over	W&T	wrap & turn (see next page)
DPN(s)	double pointed needle(s)	P	purl				
		P2tog (dec 1)	purl 2 stitches together	SKP (dec 1)	slip K-wise, knit, pass slipped stitch over	WE	work even
inc(s)	increase(s)					WS	wrong side
K	knit	P3tog (dec 2)	purl 3 stitches together	Sl	slip (see above)	WYIB	with yarn in back
K2tog (dec 1)	knit 2 stitches together			SM	slip marker	WYIF	with yarn in front
		PM	place marker	SSK (dec 1)	slip, slip, knit these 2 stitches together (see above)	YO (inc 1)	bring yarn over needle from front up over to back
K3tog (dec 2)	knit 3 stitches together	PFB (inc 1)	purl into front and back of stitch				

Jeny's Stretchy Slipknot Cast On
An extremely stretchy cast on method that does not require a long tail, great for starting top-down socks.
DIRECTIONS: Place a slip knot on needle. Make another slip knot with working yarn, but instead of placing it on needle, pull working yarn through slip knot, and place that loop on needle. Make sure this loop sits very close to previous st. Pull working yarn until new st is tight. Rep for all CO sts.

Long Tail Cast On
Fast and neat once you get the hang of it. A tutorial can be found at knitpicks.com/learning-center/learn-to-knit.

Judy's Magic Cast On
This method creates stitches coming out in opposite directions from a seamless center line, perfect for starting toe-up socks.
DIRECTIONS: Make a slip knot and place loop around one of the two needles; anchor loop counts as first st. Hold needles tog, with needle that yarn is attached to on top. In other hand, hold yarn so tail goes over index finger and yarn attached to ball goes over thumb. Bring tip of bottom needle over strand of yarn on finger (top strand), around and under yarn and back up, making a loop around needle. Pull loop snug. Bring top needle (with slip knot) over yarn tail on thumb (bottom strand), around and under yarn and back up, making a loop around needle. Pull loop snug. Cont casting on sts until desired number is reached; top yarn strand always wraps around bottom needle, and bottom yarn strand always wraps around top needle. A video tutorial can be found at knitpicks.com/video/judys-magic-cast-on.

Turkish Cast On
Another method that creates stitches coming out in opposite directions from a seamless center line, for toe-up socks.
DIRECTIONS: Make a slip knot and place it on one needle. Place two needles parallel, one on top of the other, with pointed ends facing the same direction and with slip knot loop on bottom needle. Take yarn and wrap around back, over top and back to front, looping around both needles. Make each loop to the right of the last loop. Rep until there are enough loops for half your needed CO sts, minus 1. Wrap yarn around top needle once more then bring yarn between needles. With another needle, knit sts across top needle, then knit sts across bottom needle. If using circulars, you can pull bottom needle through the loops so the loops are now on the cable and use it to knit the loops on top needle.

Stretchy Bind Off
Good basic option for binding off toe-up sock cuffs.
DIRECTIONS: K2, *insert LH needle into front of 2 sts on RH needle and knit them tog—1 st remains on RH needle. K1; rep from * until all sts have been bound off. A tutorial can be found at knitpicks.com/learning-center/sock-knitting-guide.

Jeny's Surprisingly Stretchy Bind Off (for 1x1 Rib)
A great option for binding off toe-up sock cuffs in 1x1 Rib.
DIRECTIONS: Reverse YO, K1, pass YO over; *YO, P1, pass YO and previous st over P1; reverse YO, K1, pass YO and previous st over K1; rep from * until 1 st is left, then break working yarn and pull it through final st to complete BO.

Tubular Bind Off (for 1x1 Rib)
Another good option for binding off toe-up sock cuffs in 1x1 Rib. A tutorial can be found at knitpicks.com/learning-center/tubular-bind-off.

Cables
Tutorials for different kinds of cables, including 1 over 1 and 2 over 2, with and without cable needles, can be found at knitpicks.com/learning-center/guides/cables.

Short Rows
There are several options for how to handle short rows, so you may see different suggestions/intructions in a pattern.

Wrap and Turn (W&T) (one option for Short Rows)
Work until the st to be wrapped. If knitting: Bring yarn to front, Sl next st P-wise, return yarn to back; turn work, and Sl wrapped st onto RH needle. Cont across row. If purling: Bring yarn to back of work, Sl next st P-wise, return yarn to front; turn work and Sl wrapped st onto RH needle. Cont across row. **Picking up Wraps:** Work to wrapped st. If knitting: Insert RH needle under wrap, then through wrapped st K-wise; K st and wrap tog. If purling: Sl wrapped st P-wise onto RH needle, use LH needle to lift wrap and place it onto RH needle; Sl wrap and st back onto LH needle, and P tog. A tutorial for W&T can be found at tutorials.knitpicks.com/short-rows-wrap-and-turn-or-wt.

German Short Rows (another option for Short Rows)
Work to turning point; turn. WYIF, Sl first st P-wise. Bring yarn over back of right needle, pulling firmly to create a "double stitch" on RH needle. If next st is a K st, leave yarn at back; if next st is a P st, bring yarn to front between needles. When it's time to work into double st, knit both strands tog. A video tutorial for German Short Rows can be found at knitpicks.com/video/german-short-rows.

Grafting (also known as Kitchener Stitch)
Seamlessly join two sets of live stitches together.
DIRECTIONS: With an equal number of sts on two needles, break yarn leaving a tail approx four times as long as the row of sts, and thread through a blunt yarn needle. Hold needles parallel with WSs facing in and both needles pointing to the right. Perform Step 2 on the first front st, then Step 4 on the first back st, then continue from Step 1, always pulling yarn tightly so the grafted row tension matches the knitted fabric:
Step 1: Pull yarn needle K-wise through front st and drop st from knitting needle.
Step 2: Pull yarn needle P-wise through next front st, leaving st on knitting needle.
Step 3: Pull yarn needle P-wise through first back st and drop st from knitting needle.
Step 4: Pull yarn needle K-wise through next back st, leaving st on knitting needle.
Rep Steps 1–4 until all sts have been grafted together, finishing by working Step 1 through the last remaining front st, then Step 3 through the last remaining back st. Photo tutorials can be found at knitpicks.com/learning-center/learn-to-knit/kitchener.

THIS COLLECTION FEATURES

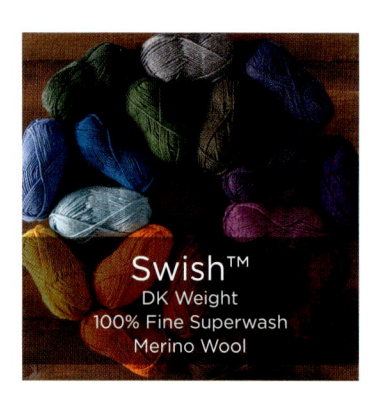

Capretta™ Superwash
Fingering Weight
80% Fine Superwash Merino Wool, 10% Cashmere, 10% Nylon

Hawthorne™ Kettle
Fingering Weight
80% Fine Superwash Highland Wool, 20% Polyamide (Nylon)

Stroll™ and Stroll™ Tonal
Fingering Weight
75% Fine Superwash Merino Wool, 25% Nylon

Stroll™ Tweed
Fingering Weight
65% Fine Superwash Merino Wool, 25% Nylon, 10% Donegal Tweed

Swish™
DK Weight
100% Fine Superwash Merino Wool

Knit Picks®

Knit Picks yarn is both luxe and affordable—a seeming contradiction trounced! But it's not just about the pretty colors; we also care deeply about fiber quality and fair labor practices, leaving you with a gorgeously reliable product you'll turn to time and time again.

View these beautiful yarns and more at
www.KnitPicks.com